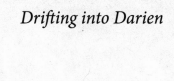

Drifting into Darien

Drifting into Darien

A PERSONAL AND NATURAL HISTORY

OF THE ALTAMAHA RIVER

Janisse Ray

The University of Georgia Press ∾ *Athens & London*

All photographs by Nancy Marshall

Published by the University of Georgia Press
Athens, Georgia 30602
www.ugapress.org
© 2011 by Janisse Ray
All rights reserved
Designed by Erin Kirk New
Set in Minion
Manufactured by Thomson-Shore and John P. Pow
    Company using 100% PCW, Processed Chlorine Free,
    acid-free, Forest Stewardship Council–certified Rolland
    Enviro100 Book paper as text stock.
The paper in this book meets the guidelines for
permanence and durability of the Committee on
Production Guidelines for Book Longevity of the
Council on Library Resources.

Printed in the United States of America

15 14 13 12 11 C 5 4 3 2 1

Library of Congress Cataloging-in-Publication Data

Ray, Janisse, 1962–
    Drifting into Darien : a personal and natural history of the
Altamaha river / by Janisse Ray.
        p. cm.
    Includes bibliographical references.
    ISBN-13: 978-0-8203-3815-6 (hardcover : alk. paper)
    ISBN-10: 0-8203-3815-x (hardcover : alk. paper)
    1. Kayaking—Georgia—Altamaha River. 2. Altamaha River
(Ga.)—History. 3. Altamaha River (Ga.)—Environmental
conditions. 4. Altamaha River (Ga.)—Description and travel.
I. Title.
    GV776.G42A577 2011
    797.122'4097587—dc23   2011021619

British Library Cataloging-in-Publication Data available

For Silas Ausable Ray-Burns

and for

Raven Wolf Mountain Reed Zapatismo Blue Waters

Contents

Preface

Me and you, river.

The Altamaha is wide and made of molasses.

It is a root doctor, gathering in her skirts alluvium and carrying these riches coastward to nurseries of shrimp and crabs. The river is a dark milk that feeds our young. Its mouth is full of baby birds.

The river is holy scripture, on which is written a creed to live by.

It is an uncertain certainty.

Along the 137 miles of the river, woods crowd both sides, the banks free of houses and lawns, for the most part—a floodplain forest in which I sometimes see the spirit of my grandfather. It is a forest of old, water-loving trees:

Water hickory.

Reams of river birch, with its silver scaling bark and its modest, tongue-shaped leaves, scratching at the sky.

Black willow, the mesh of it, the secret, the cinema.

Magnolia.

Tupelo, which I know to be hollow. My nephew Carlin looking through an open hole in a tupelo, saying, *Like a home.* The tree has pools of water in its bottom. *Even a bath*, he says. I remember loggers who chainsawed a hole in a tupelo so they could throw their cans and food wrappers inside and then replaced the block of wood to hide their mess. Imagine coming through this floodplain and discovering a trap door, what you would feel when you looked inside. A tupelo doubling as a Dumpster. A river doubling as a pipeline.

Swamp chestnut oak.

Cypress, tall and proud.

The Altamaha is a green sward, a mighty symphony of trees, an endless congress, broken only by a few bridges and trestles, a paper mill, a nuclear plant, and some effluent pipes. The river is a contradiction, breached and unbroken, nourishing and destructive, tame and wild.

The river is the same as it has been for centuries—for twenty million years—and yet it changes—another contradiction. It has two movements. One of them is geologic, a bend deepened, an oxbow forged, a bank undercut until water bursts through and forms a rushing strait. The river's other movement is current time, thousands of gallons a second rushing endlessly from the Appalachian foothills through the piedmont through the coastal plains to the sea.

Other rivers are as wide, and as dark, and as long, and as deep, and as bendy. Others are as well loved. Others are as wild.

The world is full of lively, flowing, storied rivers asking nothing, intent on their missions. Rivers both merciless and merciful.

But the Altamaha is mine, its water my blood, its history my own. I was born of it. Every drop of water I have drunk in my sojourns along it has come from it and returns to it. Thus the river informs me, as I inform it.

This river is a library, full of biota. In these stacks, everything is written in different languages. There is a dialect for motions at the surface of water, ripples and waves and minivolcanoes and sometimes only a shimmering of wind. Each species has its own vernacular, rasps and howls and bellows and flutelike songs. Fish have a lingo of puff and plop, and wild speech falls off the tongues of amphibians and reptiles. There is also a language beyond sound.

In this library, one shelf is for mussels and one is for bream that live in submerged bank roots. There is a cabinet for the life of canopies and a dictionary of grass. This library contains a reference for butterflies, a catalogue of birds. It offers a concordance of arthropods, a circulation of seeds.

The river runs and runs. It runs until it makes a circle, half in the sky, and finds itself again. It runs not simply to haul rainfall out of Georgia.

Not only to water the land.

Nor only to nourish these forests.

Nor only because it is a storehouse of life.

The river runs because it is the keeper of mystery. It is the bearer of what cannot be humanly borne. It is the course of transformation. It is a sacred urn that, once opened, changes everything.

Champion of happiness, the Altamaha is large enough to hold all joy. Creator of sorrow, it also sweeps away grief. Cradle, it rocks us into being. It is the unraveled cord of love, its tendrils reaching everywhere, finally undoing all evil.

Enter its intelligence, its love, its long dream: the back, the beyond, and the ever-flowing now.

O river, I would write your text and I would put it in the Library of People.

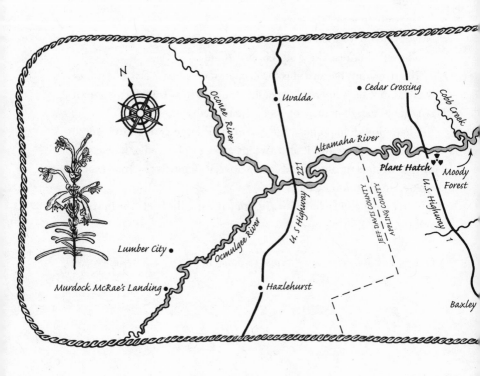

N

Oconee River

Uvalda

Cedar Crossing

Cobb Creek

Altamaha River

Plant Hatch

Moody Forest

U.S. Highway 221

JEFF DAVIS COUNTY
APPLING COUNTY

U.S. Highway 1

Lumber City

Ocmulgee River

Murdock McRae's Landing

Hazlehurst

Baxley

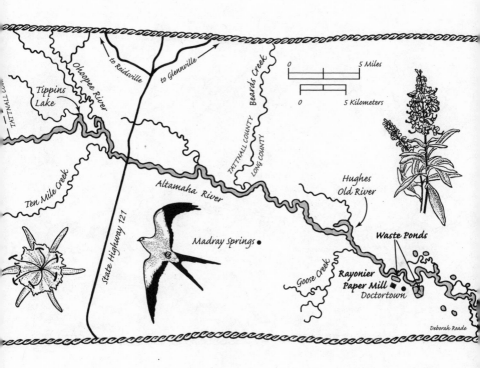

to Reidsville

to Glennville

TATTNALL COUNTY

Beards Creek

Ohoopee River

Tippins Lake

TATTNALL COUNTY
LONG COUNTY

0   5 Miles

0   5 Kilometers

Ten Mile Creek

Altamaha River

Hughes Old River

State Highway 121

Madray Springs

Waste Ponds

Goose Creek

Rayonier
Paper Mill
Doctortown

Deborah Reade

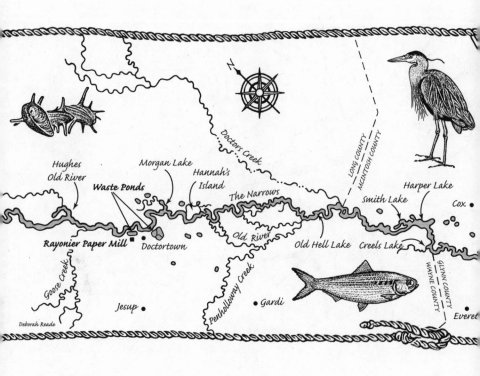

N

Doctors Creek

Hughes
Old River

Morgan Lake

Hannah's
Island

The Narrows

LONG COUNTY
MCINTOSH COUNTY

Harper Lake

Cox

Waste Ponds

Smith Lake

Rayonier Paper Mill

Doctortown

Old River

Old Hell Lake

Creels Lake

Goose Creek

Penhalloway Creek

GLYNN COUNTY
WAYNE COUNTY

Jesup

Gardi

Everet

Deborah Reade

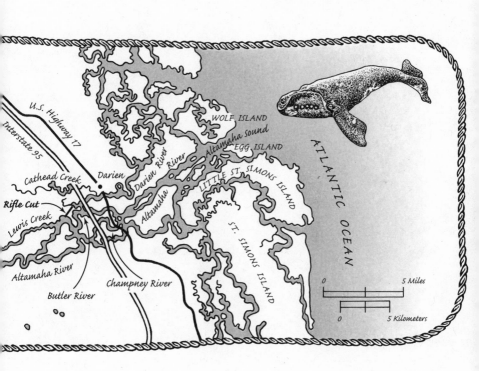

U.S. Highway 17

Interstate 95

WOLF ISLAND

Altamaha Sound

EGG ISLAND

Cathead Creek

Darien

Darien River

ATLANTIC OCEAN

Rifle Cut

Lewis Creek

Altamaha River

LITTLE ST. SIMONS ISLAND

Altamaha River

Butler River

Champney River

ST. SIMONS ISLAND

0   5 Miles

0   5 Kilometers

BOOK I

Total Immersion

Invitation

My body is a river.
Way down in the capillary of my wrist
is a little branch you can drink from.
My heart is a salty ocean, heaving back and forth,
prisoner to moon. When the blood comes in,
mullet fill my veins, so many
they are a silver thrashing bridge.
You could walk across them.

The First Day

McRae's Landing is a cleared patch of underbrush in the floodplain of the Ocmulgee River, deep south Georgia, rural and abandoned. The landing is approached by a dirt road that is littered, weedy, and eroded.

My husband and I arrive early on a Saturday morning in May, having traveled through the remote poverty of Telfair County, trying not to dwell on the events of the previous week. Fog lifts slowly off the wide, fat body of the river. The water is the color of Confederate coats. Out on the gray-blueness, a log goes floating away.

We have come bearing crosses, invisible but heavy, and if the river could pocket them, then that would be good.

A few travel trailers are set up in what look like semipermanent camps at the public landing, and two men work near one of the trailers, hoisting a motor from a truck. I roll down my window.

"Howdy! Y'all seen any canoers this morning?" Raven wants me to do the talking at times a southern accent might prove useful.

The men ratchet themselves from under the hood of the truck and rest their wrists on the fenders.

"No," one says. He's a thin man with short dark hair. "A couple of guys drove down yesterday late." That's how he talks: *yesterday late.* "They asked if this was Murdock McRae's Landing. We said we'd always known it as McRae's Landing."

The other guy, thicker with cropped auburn hair, speaks up. "Apparently Murdock McRae was a man lived in these parts a couple hundred years ago."

"Those boys said they'd be back this morning."

"We're in the right place then," I said.

"Rod Brewer," the man says. "Sorry about these hands." He holds up his grimy palms and grimaces.

"Not a problem," I say. "Glad to meet you. Looks like your work is cut out for you."

"It's always something," he says. The vernacular down here is pretty cryptic.

"And sometimes a lot at once."

"You got that right." He looks toward the boats on our truck. "What are them called?"

"Kayaks."

"So you're going out?"

"Planning on it," I say.

"How far y'all going?" Mr. Brewer asks.

"All the way to Darien, we hope."

"That's a long way."

"A week," Raven speaks up. "One hundred forty-five miles."

Mr. Brewer gazes toward the river, shining in the first rays of the sun, and a gleam strikes his dark eyes. "I've always wanted to do that," he says.

"Us too," I say.

"How many of you are making the trip?"

"Ten or twelve?" I shrug. "Well, I guess we best get unloaded."

Exactly at 8:00 a.m. a trailer chattering with loose boats rumbles up the road. I don't recognize anyone. Then another truck drives up and Dr. Presley is in it, with Crawfish and Charlie.

"Hello, hello," calls Dr. Presley. He asks how we are and we say fine, quick-like.

"Let's get launched," Dr. Presley says. "We can talk on the current."

People begin to drag boats to the riverbank and pack gear, calling back and forth. They check and double-check lists. Mr. Brewer has forsaken his mechanicking.

"You think our truck will be safe parked at the landing for a week?" I ask him.

"Don't see why not," he says pleasantly. "I've practically *lived* here for three years, and nothing I own has ever been bothered."

"You stay down here all the time?"

"Practically. I even hooked up my satellite."

∾ I know this river story has already been written. Over and over it has been told: an assemblage of people, usually men, load boats with food and fishing equipment and booze, and they step unsteadily into those boats and point their prows downstream. People see them off, and people are waiting for them at their destinations, and the people waiting will hear stories of what happened and witness the emotions on the faces of the adventurers, but those who were not transported by water will never know what really transpired.

This is just another camping-on-a-river story.

But we are different. This story includes women. I'm with my husband and a few friends and a few strangers. I'm on my favorite river in the entire world of rivers (more than 250,000 in the United States). The Altamaha is a river whose sections I have all my life swum, fished, water-skied, and floated. And now I'm slathering on sunscreen and tying a bandanna around my neck. I'm stashing a tote of fruit within reach.

Except that we're not on the Altamaha yet. The Altamaha proper is a river with unusual headwaters. It is already a giant when it starts. It begins at the confluence (a place called the Forks) of two distinct and also sizeable rivers, the Oconee and the Ocmulgee. These twin rivers rise from trickles across middle Georgia and as far north as the Brevard Fault Zone, a geologic feature that cuts above Gainesville— seeps that become branches that become creeks that become seething torrents.

Inside the great foyer of the Fernbank Museum of Natural History in Atlanta, the names of Georgia rivers are etched in Roman type in the white Georgia marble of the lintels: SATILLA, WITHLACOOCHEE, OCMULGEE, OGEECHEE, SUWANNEE. The words make a beautiful

Muscogee poem that honors history, culture, and place. The word ALTAMAHA is there. One has the feeling, looking up at the carven name, that in that marble coolness begins the ample, coffee-with-cream-colored, roiling body held within botanical banks, sliding through a beleaguered, heartbreaking, yet hopeful land.

If the shape of Georgia were a torso, the river would start in the area of the heart and lungs, then become an alimentary system, flushing out through the left kidney into Altamaha Sound on the Atlantic coast. The Altamaha's undammed main stem slices diagonally across the bottom third of the state, draining fourteen thousand square miles, almost a quarter of Georgia's land mass. Along much of it is wetland wilderness.

That the Altamaha proper is undammed should not be taken lightly. Less than 2 percent of US waterways are free-flowing for longer than 200 kilometers. That's 124 miles. Flowing freely for all 137 miles, the Altamaha is in the top 2 percent of American rivers.

To be exact, however, we have to acknowledge that the National Dam Inventory lists 276 dams in the Upper Oconee rivershed, including the impoundments, both of which loom over twenty-five feet high, that created Lake Sinclair and Lake Oconee. In addition, more than 5,400 impoundments across the entire watershed have been built across tributaries, forming irrigation ponds and other reservoirs. The full environmental impact of these mostly private dams is unstudied and underestimated.

Once when I lived in Montana, I dreamed I was back home in Georgia, working on a museum about the region. My son, Silas, was playing with rare and precious things, and I scolded him. We were hanging pictures of the river in a carpeted hall when I overheard my father say, "They're finally trying to dam the Altamaha, somewhere up near Atlanta. Some group ought to stop that." I walked off by myself up a wide corridor and began to cry. "Dam the Altamaha," I thought. "I have to stop that."

And then, in the dream, I knew my place was to fight ecologically for my home. No matter the cost.

The Altamaha's size and nature have led it to be called Georgia's Little Amazon, the most powerful river east of the Mississippi. Despite this distinction, most people remain unaware of it, which prompted Reg Murphy in his *National Geographic* article to call it "the river almost nobody knows."

For now, we are still on the Ocmulgee, referred to by the Spanish as the River of the Holy Spirit. In an hour we will reach the Forks, enter the Altamaha, and from there go drifting toward Darien.

◌ There is another reason this story is different from any other river journey. For the first time in four days, I am not scared. The river will take us away, to places roads do not go. Meanness travels roads, not rivers."Ready?"

"Ready."

"Everybody ready?" Dr. Presley calls. Boats begin to drift downstream. Dr. Presley remembers that he wants a picture, so we awkwardly pull up short and line our boats along the bank, facing the woods, while Mr. Brewer snaps a photograph and passes the camera back, apologizing again about his oily hands. We wedge our double-edged paddles against the stippled shore and push away from the lineaments of the past. Hundreds of paddlers before us have done this. So have hundreds of rafthands.

"One hundred forty-five miles to go," someone says.

"One hundred forty-five miles minus one hundred feet."

Dr. Delma Presley undebatably captains our group. He's a genteel and literate man who has one leg in the past and one in the present, plus a head full of artifacts. He taught history at Georgia Southern University, where he started a museum and from which he recently retired. Thirty or so years ago, he got the idea to construct a replica of the log rafts that wound downriver to Darien, the port on the Atlantic, from the 1870s to the 1920s, manned by poor flatwoods Crackers and black workers. Hundreds of logs, mostly of longleaf pine, journeyed to the coast lashed together. The pine was sold to buyers from northern cities and Europe, especially Great Britain, and was dispatched worldwide for use in building. Old-growth southern pine supposedly was used in construction of the USS *Constitution* (Old Ironsides); the Brooklyn Bridge; and the *Great Eastern*, which laid the first transatlantic telegraph cable. Lumber fed the economy of the Georgia coastal aristocracy.

As one verse of the folksong "Cindy" went:

Ain't gonna work in the country,
Ain't gonna work in town,
Gonna sit right here till the river rises,
And run my timber down.

"The farms of south Georgia had a cycle of life," I'd heard Dr. Presley explain in a talk at the public library in Appling County. "After the crops were laid by, the farmers could fell some of their choice trees. They built rafting into a larger cycle of life on the land."

According to Dr. Presley, 1900 marked the peak year for the timber business, when over 12.5 million board feet were officially counted.

A timber raft is an assemblage of floating logs, secured together by cross-binder poles and wooden pegs. A raft was sometimes titanic, as much as forty feet wide and two hundred feet long. The low-banked, floodplain nature of the river forbade the floating of single logs downstream because they would escape and get lost in the swamps and sloughs that insulate the river. Early rafts were constructed in squares or rectangles, but those of such design often smashed on the river bends. In the early 1870s, according to lore, a Telfair County farmer recommended crafting a raft with a pointed end, which allowed the raft to bounce off the myriad bars and bluffs. This model came to be called a "sharp shooter." Two long sweeps—one in the bow, the other at the stern, and each forty to fifty feet long—allowed for steerage.

By the 1920s, railroads and highways had all but replaced the rivers as transportation. Sometime in the early 1930s, the very last raft of all tied up in Darien.

In 1982 Dr. Presley put together crews to build and sail a commemorative Last Raft. He sweet-talked an old raftsman from Appling County, Bill Deen, ninety years old at the time and now deceased, to pilot it. Deen remembered sailing a final working float "around 1930." He told Dr. Presley that he'd guide the commemorative raft under one condition.

"What's that?" asked Dr. Presley.

"You let me call the shots," said Deen.

"It's a deal," said Dr. Presley.

"Bill Deen knew in his heart," Dr. Presley remarked later, "that this would be his last raft. He knew that on the next ride he would cross over."

The raft builders set to work, re-creating history, crafting according to a little song Bill Deen sang: "If you build it right, built it tight." Henry Eason, also of Appling County, was copilot.

When the raft set sail in the spring of 1982, eighty-one-year-old author Brainard Cheney was along. Cheney had been raised in Lumber City, Telfair County, and had attended Vanderbilt University, where he had become part of the lively literary community, the Fugitive and Agrarian movements, under way in the English department in the 1920s and 1930s. Cheney maintained lifelong friendships with Allen Tate, Andrew Lytle, Robert Penn Warren, and Flannery O'Connor. He wrote four novels, all of which are set in the wiregrass country of south Georgia and deal with themes of nature, anti-industrialism, and tradition. One of the novels, *River Rogue*, is an account of rafting.

Dr. Presley's flotilla paused at points along the way for river festivals that he organized. At these festivals people claw-hammered banjos and cooked barbecue; they churned butter, made lye soap, and quilted. Brainard Cheney read.

The raft survived its heroic voyage to Darien. Bill Deen and crew tied it up near town, on the Darien River, one of the braids of the Altamaha. It finally sank there. All of the original rafters are dead now, and what's left of the Last Raft are photographs and memories that flame in the mind of anybody who was part of that anachronistic voyage.

I missed the Last Raft. I was finishing my sophomore year at North Georgia College in Dahlonega, and getting home for a weekend, had I even known about the festival, would have been impossible. Home was six hours away, and me without wheels. I was in the mountains, enrolled in folklore, biology, and history classes, but also learning to fiddle and identify medicinals, looking for ladyslipper and trailing arbutus, panning for gold, not knowing that my home territory too was an academy.

Besides memories, one other thing remained of the Last Raft—a group called RAFTS, Rafthands of the Altamaha and Friends Together in Service. They made a ten-year reunion float trip, and again I did not hear about it. In 1992 my son was four years old, and I was in Tallahassee, trying to make my way in the world as a single mom, trying to write.

Now, twenty years later, in 2002, I have joined RAFTS, also known simply as the Rafthands. I am helping memorialize the Last Raft, re-tracing its route, and honoring the entire river and our history on it. I am not celebrating an egregious history of corporate logging. I am celebrating a culture that sprang from the flatwoods, which required a judicious use of nature, and a way of living based on the under-standing that humans without a natural landscape are dead. My fel-low boaters are paddling in plastic, wooden, and fiberglass vessels to commemorate a commemoration, celebrating great ideas and the impetus to see them through.

Tonight we will camp at Towns Bluff, because there, this after-noon, the Rafthands will hold their twentieth annual reunion with a gathering light on speeches and heavy on fried fish. It will be heavy on tall tales. It will be well attended, because many, many people feel affection for the Altamaha.

Besides Dr. Presley, two of the circa-1982 Rafthands are with us. One is John Crawford, called Crawfish by everyone who knows him, a biologist whose knowledge of southeastern natural history is boundless. He is our naturalist and our navigator, the one who laid sixteen topographical maps on the floor of his office and plotted our trip.

The other original is Charlie Reeves. Charlie builds fine kayaks— Caretta kayaks, *Caretta caretta* being the scientific binomial of the loggerhead sea turtle. In fact, Dr. Presley is riding in the Altamaha Drifter, a spectacular wooden kayak that Charlie designed and built for him. "I don't think I've ever seen a boat I didn't covet," Charlie once said to me. He's also a low-country chef, maybe a hedonist, certainly a swashbuckler who knows how to have fun.

If Crawfish is Lewis and Charlie is Clark, then I am Sacajawea. I was born ten miles south of the river in the general hospital in Baxley. I was a baby on a boat my father built that sank in the river. Strapped to a life preserver, I washed up on one of its sandbars. To celebrate my graduation from high school, my father, brother, and I took a raft trip of our own, from Lumber City down to the Highway 1 bridge, in a large boat without a motor, a plan that demonstrated our colossal ignorance of navigation. We bounced from shore to shore, carried by the whim of current. We fought snags and overhanging brush. When we anchored, the makeshift angle iron did not hold, and we woke up in a different place than where we went to sleep. But I got a story out of it.

The other boaters, twenty or so, I haven't met. Many of them will end their trip at the reunion later today. Eight of us will sail the river to its mouth, and by that point we will know each other as if we were family.

None of us talks much at first. We get accustomed to the murmuration of the paddles, water dripping off blades. We take in the indigo of the water, the chartreuse of spring leaves. It's the third of May, and the floodplain is reborn. In an architecture this beautiful, the cypress needles new, religious conversions are possible. We settle into the feel of our boats, our cushions, our backrests. We look around at each other and paddle along, partial and sometimes whole smiles on our faces, thinking, *So this is what free feels like.* And others, *This is holy.* I am thinking, *At last, I am far away and getting farther from all that is bad in the world.*

I'm not, really. But for a while, traveling through the desolate forests of rural Telfair, I feel as if I am.

The river rises, fed by rainstorms as far north as the capital.

We have journeyed a half mile when I hear and spot a kingfisher. I start a bird list. No. 1: belted kingfisher. A large woodpecker breaststrokes across the sky, and I snatch up my binoculars. Pileated. Call me nuts, but I am looking for an ivorybill. The ivorybilled woodpecker was, or is, a thirty-inch-wingspan, black-and-white bird once found in the Altamaha swamps. The Altamaha was the last place that renowned naturalist Herbert Stoddard saw an ivorybill. My friend the ecological forester Leon Neel told me the story. Mr. Stoddard was in Florida woods one day in 1952 when he saw two ivorybilled woodpeckers, both females. "You won't believe what I just saw," he said to Leon later. The next morning they were in the swamp at 4:00 a.m. According to Leon, for the next few months he and Mr. Stoddard stayed in the swamp, searching. Years later, Mr. Stoddard saw the last one of his life. He was in a plane that detoured around a thunderstorm, and as he crossed over the Altamaha River, he saw a woodpecker perched in a cypress. Then it flushed and he saw that indeed it was an ivorybill. Leon said that Mr. Stoddard believed in protecting the resource and never reported his sighting in any ornithological journal. "I'm afraid they're gone," Mr. Stoddard had told him.

Hope, however, for the ivorybill has not been entirely extinguished. And there's no harm in looking.

I catch up to Crawfish, who is in a canoe and on vacation from his work at the University of Georgia Marine Education Center on Skidaway Island. Raven slips in on the port side.

"We're sticking with *you*," I say.

"How did I get so lucky?" Crawfish says. He is incredibly good-natured.

"You know everything."

"Don't count on it," he says.

"What's the chance of seeing an ivorybill?"

"Well, you never know," he says.

More than 120 rare or endangered species can be found in the basin of the Altamaha River. Forty-three of them are imperiled, including the Atlantic sturgeon, swallow-tailed kite, American oyster-catcher, and spiny mussel. Also including Alabama milkvine, Radford's mint, and the only Georgia population of Florida cork-wood. I want to see imperiled things.

Crawfish points out tracks of softshell turtles on sandbars and the homes of bank swallows in clay banks. He identifies bird-voiced tree frogs and bullfrogs. Red-shouldered hawk, spotted sandpiper, Mississippi kite, wood duck—the bird list grows quickly. But no ivorybill.

〜 I am newly married to Raven, six weeks now. I have moved from my grandmother's farm near the Altamaha to live with him in his log home down a narrow, moss-draped, white-sand driveway deep in the deciduous woods of Wakulla County, Florida, near the village of Crawfordville. Raven is a letter carrier.

In a way, this river trip is our honeymoon, although our heads are too confused to feel as if we are honeymooning.

Earlier this week a law enforcement officer showed up at our door. I was home alone when he arrived, and I watched him stride through monkey grass and up onto the wide pine porch. When he knocked I thought for a minute he was going to separate the door from its hinges.

"Can I help you?" I smiled.

The deputy frowned. He demanded to know where my husband was. I told him Raven was at the Adams Street post office in Talla-hassee, sorting mail for delivery, but that soon he would be out on his route and hard to find. I asked about the nature of the officer's visit.

"You'll find out soon enough," he said brusquely.

"Has someone committed a crime?" I asked.

He snorted. "You're asking me?"

"You don't have to be mean," I told him. "Whatever you think my husband has done didn't happen."

"We'll see," he said. He glared at me and left.

The cruiser was no sooner gone than the phone rang.

"I've heard that the police are looking for me," Raven said.

"One was just here," I said.

"What did he say?"

"Nothing," I said. "He wouldn't talk to me. He was pretty rude, actually."

"I heard that it's not only the police but the Florida Department of Law Enforcement. I'm going to their office."

"Whose?"

"The FDLE."

"What is all this about?" I asked.

"I don't know," he said.

"I'm coming in to be with you." Tallahassee was sixteen miles away. "I'll meet you at the FDLE."

On the way I picked up my friend Susan Cerulean, the writer. We've been friends for over two decades and have seen each other through some hard times, and no doubt we will see each other through more to come. "We seem," she once said to me, "to be plugging the holes in each other's hearts."

By the time she and I whipped into law enforcement headquarters, 1:15 p.m., Raven was being questioned, so the receptionist said.

"Can we go where he is?" I asked.

"No, that's not possible."

"Can you get a message to him to come out?"

"I can try."

"Will you do that?"

"I'll try."

We waited in a cold room made mostly of glass, where sofas and chairs had been placed back to back. Outside, people sat on concrete benches, smoking. Ten minutes passed. I approached the front desk.

"Have you been able to reach my husband?"

"He is being questioned. I can't get a message to him."

"This is important. We need to speak with him."

"What is this about?" she asked.

"I have no idea."

"I don't think I should interrupt them."

"Is he safe?"

"Of course."

"Will you try again?"

"I'll try."

"Thank you," I said.

While we waited, Susan and I contemplated getting an attorney. We began to thumb through the yellow pages. After a half hour we made a decision. We would give the interrogation another fifteen minutes. Then we would simply begin to keen. I petitioned the receptionist again. With ten minutes to spare before the wailing began, she reached Raven by telephone in a locked room.

"Will they let you leave?" I asked him.

"I'm not being held," he said. "Just questioned."

"What is this about?"

"I'll explain it to you."

"This seems a lot like imprisonment to me. You're behind locked doors where nobody can get to you."

He was quiet.

"I don't understand what's going on," I said. "But whatever this is about, it's serious. You need an attorney, you need not to say another word without one."

"They say I can go anytime."

"Then leave," I said. "I'm in the waiting room upstairs."

Ten minutes later Raven emerged.

I grabbed him and we hugged a long time. Susan had her hand on his back. "What happened?" I said.

Raven's eyes welled with tears. He glanced around the dull lobby, where people waited in stony silences. "We can't talk here," he said.

The police had been looking for Raven all weekend. We had been away, at a gathering of southern nature writers. The police had interviewed other people associated with Raven, including colleagues at work.

Someone had written a death threat to the governor of Florida. It was typed, one line, but one line is all that's needed to disrupt a life, to crush a heart. Even now, I can hardly bear to write what the letter said.

"Dear Mr. Bush. Your not a responsible man so I am going to kill you."

The typed signature on the misspelled letter was my husband's birth name, not the nickname he usually used.

At first the investigators had been intimidating, Raven said, and they wouldn't tell him why they had wanted to speak with him. When the postal inspector showed up, Raven knew the problem was serious. Had someone seen him peeing out his delivery van? Had he misdelivered an important package?

The investigators read my husband his rights and began questioning: Did he hate the governor? (No, he said.) Did he disagree with the governor's politics? (Sometimes.) Had he written a death threat to the governor? (No.)

Another piece of information is vital to this story. Raven worked a downtown mail route in Tallahassee. Although the Capitol was on his route and he often sorted mail for it, he never delivered there. The Capitol gets so much mail that it requires a special carrier. However, if Raven had sorted the mail on the day the letter was sent, or the day it was delivered to the Capitol, his fingerprints would have decorated the envelope.

After a number of questions and an equal number of Raven's honest answers, the investigators admitted that the letter writing was obviously a hate crime not against the governor but against Raven himself. They changed tactics. Did he have any enemies?

"I can't think of anyone," Raven said.

"We'll still have to do a lie-detector test."

"Not now," Raven said. "I'm too upset. I'll come back."

Who was our enemy? Who could have written the letter?

My husband wrangled a doctor's excuse not to return to work immediately. We were filled beyond belief with sadness and fear that left us exhausted. Who could have done this terrible thing? What would happen to us? We examined all our relationships. Raven had been waiting on a quitclaim deed from someone who was slow in presenting it. A neighbor (and friend) had pointed out that part of our driveway, a piece of earth about the size of a baby blanket, appeared to cross the property line, and we were in the process of surveying the line. I had been speaking out against the Hatch Nuclear Plant on the Altamaha. As a member of the board of Altamaha Riverkeeper I had testified against a tire manufacturer that had dumped copper and arsenic into the river, and the company had gone bankrupt before it could be held accountable. But the letter didn't have my name on it.

In our new-marriage bliss and in our connectedness, however, we felt as if the crime had been waged against us both. It might even have been an attack on our happiness, which was enormous.

Looking back, our response to the incident is what most interests me. Plenty of people have lived lives under menace, and the threats have been more direct, more violent, more frightening. Many have lived through events much more terrifying—armed robbery, for example. Even unarmed robbery. Why, then, in the days following the interrogation, did we wake up crying and go to bed crying? Most of us, I believe, give our lives away to fear. Knowing that, there I was, nonetheless paralyzed.

Wangari Maathai, in interviews with her filmmaker, Lisa Merton, talked about fear. "If you have fear," she said, "it has to be there in you and you have to discover it in you. It has to influence your thoughts. You have to see danger. If you don't see danger, you'll do anything. And I have never been in a position where I see danger. I guess that's what makes it possible for me to keep going because I do not visualize danger. . . . Fear comes from imagining—you foresee what is likely to happen to you."

Fear is what stops most of us in our tracks: fear of ridicule, fear of hunger, fear of failure. The greatest among them is fear of death.

"But if you do not foresee the damage that is likely to happen to you and you only see the good that you are likely to do, then you can go through wars and people wonder where you get the energy," said Maathai. "I don't know what courage is. Whatever it is, I don't see it as courage. I see it as pursuing what I know is possible."

A more rational response on our part to the letter writing, I believe, would have been to mull over the events; decide what, if anything, could be done about them; do it; and go on with our lives. Keep thinking of all the good that we were likely to do.

Years later we would become better adapted to handle the abject fear. But not yet. We were newly wed; we were living halcyon days swept up in the sweetness of finally having found each other. All our lilies were gilded.

Meanwhile, detectives asked to test our manual typewriter, to compare its font with that in the letter, which washed in more fear. We often left our home unlocked. Had someone come in and used our typewriter? Who was that someone?

We commenced to locking doors. We were careful at night. If the telephone rang, both of us answered, one from each of two phones, one speaking and the other silent, listening for clues. Somewhere we had an enemy, and that enemy was angry enough to try to send one of us to jail.

We needed an oculus, a god's eye. To stare down the evil.

We could have cancelled the river trip. Instead, we informed the investigators that we would be out of town for ten days. We packed camping gear. On the river, would more evil find us? Would investigators follow us? Would we be able to forget and forgive?

Our voyage began.

꩜ Since I became a member of RAFTS, I have joined another organization important to the river.

In December 1998 I attended a state-run public hearing in Jesup, Georgia, regarding water quality in the Altamaha. At the meeting I was introduced to an idea that had been percolating in the mind of one James Holland, a crabber on the coast. Holland had been watching his catch dwindle, year after year, and the more reading he did on the subject and the more meetings he attended, the more he connected the devastation of a fishery with the quality of water upstream.

He stood up in the hearing. "What are you doing about non-point-source pollution?" he asked the Environmental Protection Division officials. "Why aren't you testing water quality in the estuary, where we depend on it for a living?"

I looked around the room, amazed. Although the Altamaha is huge, up to that point it had been largely ignored by science and by government and sometimes by its own citizenry. But more than thirty people had shown up to the Jesup meeting.

Who they were shocked me more. These weren't well-heeled, college-educated, liberal idealists. They were manual laborers. They dressed in boots and work clothes. They loved to fish for shad.

And they were pissed off. They'd seen too many degradations of the river, they were quick to tell the state officials—increased pollution and sediment and algae and exotic species—and they were tired of the EPD not doing its job.

My young son, Silas, was with me, and because it was a school night, we left early. A man got up and followed us to the car.

"Hey," he said. He had clear blue eyes and short dark hair. "I can see you're interested in the river. I got up off the front row to chase you down."

"What did I do to deserve that?"

"Just acted interested," he said. "Where are you from?" he asked.

"Baxley," I said.

"We're going to do something about the river," he said. "We've got a grant to start a group and we need people from up your way to get involved."

"I'm definitely sympathetic," I said. "But I can't stay tonight because it's past bedtime now."

"Give me some way to contact you," he said, "and I'll keep you posted on our first meeting."

The card he handed me said "Robert DeWitt, R&R Seafood."

Little did I know then that a handful of citizens had started meeting in the Darien office of Christi Lambert, who works for The Nature Conservancy to protect the Altamaha River and coastal Georgia. Concerned about the river, together they figured out they could start a Riverkeeper group.

How simple events transform our lives fascinates me. It's a normal day, just another meeting, another person on the street. We look back and marvel. "That was a fork in the road," we realize. "I took one path and it has made all the difference."

By mid-January I was in Darien, a small coastal town, one of more than a dozen people meeting along the riverfront. It was a memorable and groundbreaking occasion. James Holland ran the meeting. He wore his dark hair slicked back at the hairline, revealing a forehead deeply grooved by twenty years on a crab boat. He was a big, vehement man with hands to match his body and eyes unnerving in their intensity. He looked like someone not to cross.

"My reason for being here is greed," he said. "I'm a crabber. And I'm watching my way of living going down the drain. From live coral reefs on up, marine life is being destroyed by what we do upriver."

Robert DeWitt was equally emphatic. "I grew up on the river," he said, "and now I run a seafood business. I've seen the river come from one of the most productive shad fisheries to no shad fishery."

Water quality in the basin had been declining steadily. Nutrient levels in the delta had more or less doubled in thirty years. These nutrients are nitrates and phosphates formed from nitrogen and phosphorus, which enter the river from agricultural and silvicultural runoff, as well as wastewater treatment plants and sewage systems. The nutrients cause excessive plant growth, including phytoplankton and algae, as well as plant decay, which leads to decreases in dissolved oxygen, suffocating fish and other riverine and marine life.

Water quality is also diminished by clear-cutting along stream banks, altered drainage patterns, and point-source pollution, meaning pollution that can be traced back to a single source.

Yes, we would start a protection group. We would join the Riverkeeper movement. We would *reverse the damage*.

Altamaha Riverkeeper would be based on Hudson Riverkeeper, a watchdog organization founded in 1966 by commercial fishers determined to improve water quality in the nearly dead Hudson. Since 1983, when they hired a full-time riverkeeper, John Cronin (whom I have since met), Hudson Riverkeeper has forced hundreds of violators to spend over one billion dollars to clean up their acts. Independent groups nationwide have followed the Hudson model, and together they now form the Waterkeeper Alliance, two hundred strong.

After our first meeting I stood outside in the sunshine with Holland. About a quarter mile away the Altamaha threaded through salt marsh. "We're gonna take that river back," Holland said. "It belongs to the people." At that moment, he told me later, he was the happiest man alive.

Things were rolling from the start. We put together a board. Within a week the board adopted a mission and a set of by-laws, and then elected officers. Holland located office space, distributed membership forms, and applied for nonprofit status. We sent out press releases with our brand-new hotline, 1-877-ALTAMAH.

Within six weeks Altamaha Riverkeeper had 125 members. With a smidgen of money we hired an executive director, Deborah Sheppard, a stalwart, knowledgeable, and devoted advocate who had moved from Atlanta to Darien for a simpler lifestyle. James Holland was named Altamaha Riverkeeper.

While Deborah kept the organization solvent and steady, Holland got out in the basin. He spoke the people's language, talking to garden and Rotary and Lions and hunt clubs; to chambers of commerce; to college, high school, and elementary classes; to city councils and county commissions. He went to Atlanta, to Athens, to Dublin, to Brunswick, to Jesup. He went to Hazlehurst, Ludowici, Macon, Lumber City, Everett City. To Savannah, Baxley, Odum, Gardi. Up and down the river, in and out of the watershed he went.

One of the first things he learned was how big the watershed is. Protecting the river wouldn't simply mean the main artery. It would mean every capillary and vein: Alex Creek, Alligator Creek, Battle Creek, Beards Creek, Bells Mill Creek, Buckhorn Creek, Bullard Creek, Cathead Creek, Cobb Creek, Doctors Creek, Five Mile Creek, Gardi Creek, Goose Creek, Goose Run Creek, Grantham Lake, Griffin Lake, Inside Lake, Johnson Lake, Jones Creek, Lewis Creek, Little Alligator Creek, Little Creek, Little Doctors Creek, Little Goose Creek, Little Rocky Creek, Little Ten Mile Creek, Morgan Lake, Milligan Creek, Moody Creek, Mushmelon Creek, Oconee Creek, Penholloway Creek, Pico Creek, Rocky Creek, Slaughter Creek, S. Prong Beards Creek, Studhorse Creek, Ten Mile Creek, Thomas Creek, Walker Creek, Watermelon Creek, Watson Creek, Whaley Lake, Wiggins Lake, Williams Creek. And many more. It would mean every water thread flowing into the Oconee and Ocmulgee. It would mean the unnamed creeks and sloughs as well.

"This sucker is mammoth," Holland said.

As he traveled, he watched over the river, like a guardian angel. He found good things—people who cared, who had been educated to understand that bombardments on nature are aggressions against human beings, who comprehended that a river is only as healthy and intact as its forests.

But everywhere Holland went—testing waters with his kits, for fecal coliform and worse—he saw bad things, too, and he took pictures. A blackwater creek ruined by logging, a slough choked with construction and demolition material. A town's sewage pipe, stringy stuff hanging from vegetation downstream. He'd send the pictures to the rest of us. "Y'all be the judge and the jury," he wrote.

He had two good feet, he had a truck, he had a boat. Private property would stop him, he learned after an overnight in a Cochran jail, but nothing else.

He sent pictures of the Rayonier paper mill discharge pipe, images of foam and purple water. A year later he sent more pictures. He met with Rayonier. After many years he e-mailed more pictures—"Still nasty as all hell," he wrote.

He visited another discharge point. "It smells like soap around this pipe," he wrote. "Maybe they call soapy water clean water?"

He tested a creek immediately downstream of a dairy farm. The fecal coliform count was 24,000 colonies per one hundred milliliters (safe contact for humans is 200 colonies).

In February forty people attended an informational meeting in Baxley. They talked about how the sandbars used to be white as sugar and now they're stained by algae, how the previous summer the algae was so thick the water looked like spinach stew, how the river was more shallow than it had ever been because of sediment build-up, how they were scared to eat the fish.

The pictures kept coming: clear-cutting, illegal boat ramps, a beheaded alligator floating belly up, a deer carcass in the water, improper stream crossing during timber operations, deep rutting, illegal ditching, a stream destroyed by a road. With the pictures came Holland's comments: "Shame on the person who did this" and "How to ruin a perfect day." And, "He needs to be in jail along with his cohorts and if I can help him get there I will sleep good at night."

No polluter or destroyer could hide, and when they tried, with beauty strips and backwoods abominations and No Trespassing signs, Holland took to the air. SouthWings, an environmental flying service based in Asheville, North Carolina, flew him over the basin many times, whenever he needed to examine from the air something that could not be seen from the ground.

Altamaha Riverkeeper began to litigate and to win. The river began to win. A people began to reconcile themselves with their landscape, with their home, and with each other. A people began to reconcile themselves with God.

It happened so quickly, a new environmental community that had seemed light-years away. By summer the organization listed two hundred people as members.

〰 A group of defenders now one thousand strong is sticking up for the river. The Altamaha has a family now, it has a community, it has support. Invisible though they are, these riverkeepers give me comfort as I cruise along on my journey. The day is hot, low nineties, and we keep covered with sleeves and hats. Our roof is the occasional cumulus cloud, our walls the trees. We are cradled in a womb of water.

By midmorning we arrive at the confluence: the Forks.

The Oconee tumbles out of Georgia from the direction of Athens and Milledgeville, itself formed from two rivers, the Upper Oconee and the Middle Oconee; and the Ocmulgee rolls out of Atlanta and Macon, gathering the waters of the Yellow, the South, and the Alcovy. The two waterbodies ram into each other in a remote forest unreachable by public road, near the juncture of Montgomery, Wheeler, and Jeff Davis counties. The towns nearest the Forks are Hazlehurst and Lumber City. The point of origin for many rafts, Lumber City was home of the largest sawmill in the South when the town was incorporated in 1881.

The Forks is a dark vortex. The air zings with energy. The water is disgruntled. It no longer flows but roils and storms. The rivers don't make a Y, they make a T. A freshet in one tributary holds the other at bay. With much grumbling and fighting, the waters finally merge and form a wide, slow, meandering body.

When Hernando de Soto came through in 1540 looking for precious metals, he called the river Altama. Since *al* in Spanish means "to," "Altama" would mean "way to Tama." (Oliver Goldsmith repeats the name Altama in his 1770 poem "The Deserted Village.") Historians assumed that Tama was a Creek village located at the confluence, although that theory is now refuted. Maybe the settlement was on the Ocmulgee. Maybe the tribe was the Yemassee, not the Creek. Perhaps, modern archaeologists say, Tama was a territory, not a village.

Nobody knows. The origin of the name is one of many, many stories lost to history.

Interestingly, on another map drawn during the Spanish era, the river is called Rio de Telaje, *telaje* meaning "pasturage for grazing."

Still, artifacts *have* been found at the Forks, and it is a power spot, a kind of sacred place encountered only occasionally on the pulsing globe. I know the man who owns this holy ground, and I hope that one day he will protect it from vilification.

Raven and I lag behind the other paddlers, some of whom never stop to rest or sightsee. We bank and wander into the woods, like children, exploring deep in the slough, touching the trunks of huge tupelos and shiny-barked sycamores. I get to introduce my new husband to all this. A few cypress knees stand taller than we do. We find a turtle skeleton. Carolina chickadees hang like trapeze artists from Virginia creeper. Pishing—making the repeated sound of *pish* that produces a buzz to attract birds because it mimics their alarm call—Raven sees his first prothonotary warbler, the bright yellow canary of the swamp.

"That's a male. The females are much more drab," I say to him. "You men."

"All show," he says.

"I haven't cried in twenty-four hours," I say.

"Are you saying that because you're happy, or because you need to?"

I burst into tears, and he puts his arms around me. We stand in holiness, in beauty, safe and sound.

Here the Altamaha River starts. Here our journey begins, toward trust, toward forgiveness. In 137 river-miles, surely a tortured mind can find peace.

Before we trek any farther, let's get the pronunciation of the river correct. And the spelling too, while we're working on technique. We pronounce the word ALL-tuh-muh-HAW. The predominant stress is on the last syllable, although the first is also stressed, the middle two barely at all. (A lot of people say All-tuh-MA-ha, but that is not right.) An early spelling of the word that is still sometimes seen is Alatamaha, as in Gordonia Alatamaha State Park in Reidsville. The pronunciation is the same, the second vowel silent.

Back on the water, I contemplate the vessels that have traveled where I am passing, from cypress dugouts as much as eleven thousand years ago, to Spanish craft, to poleboats, to rafts of timber and cotton, to paddle-wheel steamboats, to motorized bass boats, to our plastic kayaks. In the recesses of my mind I can almost see this historic parade. What has remained constant, thus far, is the river itself, engaged in its lifelong mission of executing the water cycle, filling and releasing, taking and giving, rising and falling, absorbing and evaporating.

At Round Bluff, a swallow-tailed kite swoops low over the trees. It appears from the port side of the floodplain and pirouettes in yellow sunlight. If you've never seen a swallow-tailed kite, you must go as soon as possible to find one. You must get in a boat on a river where they can still be found and keep watching the sky. The swallow-tailed kite is the most beautiful bird of all.

Its wingspan is almost four feet. It has distinctive markings, black wings and a white belly and head; its black tail is deeply forked, which allows it unusual aerial abilities. It swoops and pivots, spins and dives. It glides across the old floodplain forests, twigs in beak, building a nest high in the top of the tallest tree emerging from the canopy. It snaps insects midair.

This is a rare bird. Historically occurring in seventeen states, as far north as Wisconsin, at the dawn of the twenty-first century this bird has a population of less than five thousand, with a breeding population of eight hundred to twelve hundred pairs, and is found only in seven southeastern states. Prior to 1997, one nest had been documented in Georgia, but since, biologists have located and monitored more than two hundred.

If you go out on the Altamaha River, where kite nests have been found, between March and July, you may see one. Toward the end of July the birds begin amassing in huge flocks, foraging relentlessly for their coming migration to South America, diving for June bugs and dragonflies. They congregate in mowed fields in Tattnall and Long counties; sometimes you can see more than one hundred in a flock. By the first of August they are gone again, back to Brazil, where they overwinter. (More accurately, they live in Brazil and oversummer with us.) When they are gone, we miss them. The day they arrive back, another spring, we celebrate.

Late afternoon more bad news spills out of the big world. When we approach Towns Bluff (also called Warehouse Landing), just below the Highway 221 bridge, where the reunion will be held, we see a fire truck and police cruisers and lots of people. It looks as if a festival is under way—the fire truck has come out for the kids to climb on, police monitor the crowds.

The closer we drift, however, the less festive the atmosphere seems. There's even a car from the Georgia Bureau of Investigation.

Oh no, Raven is thinking. I have been descending into the same whirlpool. *They have followed us here.*

But no. News passes mouth to mouth: search-and-rescuers look for the body of a nine-year-old boy who drowned in the afternoon, going after a ball. His father, we hear, tried to save him and almost drowned himself, entangled in a trot line. Boats with weighted nets are dragging the river bottom, men standing in them wielding grappling hooks. An officer leads a search dog up and down the bank. The family of the boy has congregated in tight knots, stunned looks on faces.

We bank at Towns Bluff, turning our backs to the tragedy and turmoil and shifting our attention toward the engulfing aromas of frying fish. Welcome to the Twentieth Rafthands Reunion.

Rafthands of the Altamaha and Friends Together in Service (RAFTS) was a historical society. Anybody interested in preserving the river's traditions was welcome to become a member. All you did was send in ten bucks for dues. I first heard of it in 1998 from Christi Lambert of The Nature Conservancy's Altamaha Bioreserve Project. I wrote to then-president Jeff Dukes, who sent me a sample issue of the *Rafthands Holler*, whose name is derived from the eerie, haunting calls made up and down the river at sunrise and sunset by the rafthands. I became Rafthand Janisse.

The year following the epic Last Raft from Murdock McRae's Landing to Darien, in 1983, the crew and their friends met beneath the span of the Uvalda Bridge. RAFTS met every May for the next quarter-century. The reunion was mainly a chance for friends to gather. The potluck meal was long, featuring fish caught and cooked by Rafthands Mike and Helen Stewart of Hazlehurst, and the business meeting was short. Nay votes were voiced with "No way!" and ayes with "Why not?"

Because the group honored a historical way of life, and because, let's face it, fewer and fewer people have time to care about yester-year at all, and because history slides ever farther into the past, the Rafthands were always dealing with loss and grief. At almost at every reunion a ceremony had to be performed honoring someone who had died. "We pause to remember and to respect the memory of Rafthands who have gone down to the sea and have crossed over to the other side. We miss them." Then someone motored out and launched a biodegradable wreath midstream.

In the early days, real-life rafters showed up. In May 1999, the *Holler* recognized Ed Towns and Barney Goodman, the last remaining real rafthands. At the May 2000 reunion Howard Reddish of Wayne County introduced himself and said, "I'm eighty-nine years old and, thank the Lord, my daddy let me go rafting with him when I was a boy, around 1930." Rafthand widows showed up, chocolate cakes in hand. Sometimes nearly one hundred people assembled.

After the last of the whipped cream is scraped from our plates, after the "fun, fellowship, and feasting," after the final "Why not?", after the cleanup is done, sixteen of us climb back in boats and float a few miles downstream, to Half Moon Round, where we will camp. Everybody is thinking of the lost boy. We are looking for him. Nobody wants to find a body, though all of us want him found.

Our sun sets on the first day. We have come twenty miles.

Raven and I pitch our tent away from the others, our zip-lock door facing east, and we hold each other through a spring night wracked by the hoarse cries of nocturnal life.

The Second Day

On Sunday morning everybody is up earlier than I expect. Sixteen people continue, although later today the employed will disembark to return to work and eight of us will push on. An hour after I hear the first hiss of a stove and clank of cups, I'm still in the tent. Troubled by dreams, I wake sad, as if in the big world anything could be happening that we should know about. Our fourteen-year-old son, Silas, is still in school in Vermont—is he OK? Are our parents hale? Was the little lost boy found?

I feel grooves in my face. I have a lump in my throat all the way down to my stomach.

Raven climbs out and stands, beautiful and happy, in front of the tent, looking around at Half Moon Round. No house or road or any human construction mars the view. The fat, orange sun comes up over a misty river. Earth has made another revolution.

"Good morning," Charlie calls.

Raven returns the greeting.

"Do you know what zip code this is?" Charlie is thinking how happy Raven must be not to be at work. Nobody knows about the letter.

Raven grins. "Not a mailbox around."

We embark around nine and face a burly headwind all morning.

~ When I was a young woman, I learned how to meditate, but I've never been very good at it. Sit quietly and still your mind, I was taught. Begin by paying attention to your breathing. Watch your breath, they said. Watch it go in and watch it go out. If your mind wanders, watch it wander and bring it back to your breath.

I think if I'd been a more proficient meditator, I could have graduated from breath watching to switch flipping: sitting down and shutting off the mind. But I've got a mind like a jumping jack, bouncing all over. I've got a mind like a thousand hobos. I'm not lying to you, I tried to meditate. I sat and followed my breath as it went in and out. To me, it was a lot like sleeping, except sleep is more efficient.

The river itself seems to be meditating and having as hard a time of it as I. On the surface it flows peacefully, but in its mind I know there's mayhem. It's restless, chattering ceaselessly.

The only way I've been able to meditate is to sit in nature. There, the mind of the river floods my own and emancipates me. That happens now, as we undulate through our first propitious miles. I fill my lungs with oxygen-rich air saturated with the first honeysuckle and the promise of blackberries, with clay dust and gasses bubbling from black muck. I am free.

᷍ Six miles later, just past McMatt Falls, we reach Benton Lee's Steakhouse, and my mind is racing again, full of static.

Until the American Revolution, the Altamaha was the western border of the colony of Georgia, and land below the river remained closed to white settlers. The southerly holdings belonged to Creek Indians, who lived in settlements farther upstream, using the river as transportation and the surrounding territory as hunting grounds. The river was the line of demarcation between open and closed, white and native, as settlers pushed south from North Carolina and Virginia, and inland from the coast, homesteading the north side of the river.

Rafters came to refer to the riverbanks as the "white" side or the "Indian" side. "Bow white" and "Bow Injun" were common cries.

Slowly, white settlers began to cross the river and claim more frontier from the natives, who were decimated by European diseases and who saw their empires falling. In the early 1800s whites poured across. In 1838 the majority of the Creek Indians were driven to Oklahoma on the terrible Trail of Tears, although pockets of natives remained, holed up in swamps and bays, or on private land.

We had planned to have a big steak dinner at Benton Lee's, which is located at Gray's Landing, on the "white" side of the river. Benton Lee's dishes up grotesquely huge steaks—the big ones will completely cover a sheet of legal paper. It's one of those places that serves a steak so big, if you can consume all of it, you get it free.

Most of us have lost our appetite for steak. We order sandwiches and refill water jugs and relish the luxury of the bathroom. Raven and I check phone messages—there are none—and call Silas, who wishes he were with us. I introduce myself to a man named Lee who is from Atlanta and works for a magazine. He joined the trip this morning and will be with us overnight.

"Are you writing a story?" I ask.

"I'm here to fish," he says. "If I get a story, that'll be bonus."

When we relaunch, we are traveling toward the part of the river I know best. These waters of my home ground are drenched with memories, with stories. As I paddle I think of my paternal grandfather, Charley, a muscular, barrel-chested man not quite six feet tall who by fate had been orphaned at a young age, a turn of events that caused him lifelong trouble. He'd been thrown to the winds of the world at thirteen and had found in the woods not only a home but also his livelihood and sustenance.

He was a husband and a father of eight when his mental illness became unbearable, and my grandmother had him institutionalized in Milledgeville, in the state mental hospital. But one day he escaped. He got out a door and down to the Oconee River, and he jumped in the river and sank. He swam and swam.

After a long way he crawled out on a bank and rested. His shoes were full of water, and his wet britches and shirt stuck to his skin. But his mind was clear. The world was glittering and bright, and he was glad to be in it. He slid back in the water.

This was the 1940s. The man in the river, my headstrong and reckless grandfather, moved southeast, downstream, with the current, keeping to edges and banks, circling around fisherpeople. Night came and he found a place to sleep. When the sun broke the next morning, he spread his clothes to dry and sought berries. Later that day near a landing he noodled for catfish and brought one up, then hustled fire from a nearby farm.

For two months he made his way thus down the Oconee to the Forks, then down the Altamaha, headed home. For the kind of man my grandfather was—edgy, wild, violent, even dangerous—two months in the river floodplain was nothing. He was a survivor. He knew how to make it. He met farmers in their valley fields. He met two criminals on the lam, living in a hollow tupelo. Maybe he met a black bear.

When he got to one of the landings closest to Baxley he solicited a ride to town, spent one night there, and left for the orange groves of Florida. When I was thirteen, I began a correspondence with my grandfather. I still have the letters, return address a rural route in Wauchula, Florida. Charley was seventy-five years old and had just married his second wife, also a septuagenarian, whom I never met.

Here is one of his letters. In it my grandfather is concerned that his tiny Social Security check has been cut because of his marriage, and he has decided to get a divorce. There is no punctuation.

page 1
I will ancer your letter I was sure glad to hear from you we are all well at my house I planing on moving out by my self they have cut my check to 44 dollars we can't make it on that Claime I owe them 11 hundred dollars I don't see how that I can make it we are braking up I am going some place els I don't know where we are stoping living to gether on a no fault just checks cut I was getting 167.80 now just 44 I hope all of you are well I am ok at present time

page 2
I have tamed 3 squarles that I have tamed I can call them down a tree and feed out of my hand they are 4 are 5 babys one wont come down to eat it come down to day but got scared and back up the tree it was smaller than the tame ones ½ as big say I will hatch of some bidies and ship them to you if you wont some I have 4 hens that lay green

eggs if you wont some I will ship them to you say 1 pig is growing
now it was wild but I tame now was a dog that was wild I tamed him.

page 3
Wander [my first cousin, Wanda] likes him now he is solid jet black
with long pretty hair I am think of caring my boat and motor to the
coast and go toward Brunswick Ga till I find good fishing place and
build me a fishing shack and sell fish I belive I would like that I have a
nice present far you if no one goes up there soon I will mail it to you
well I will stop for now tell all hello for me and rite when you can and
all the news BY BY for now from GrandPA Charley J. Ray

I was too young then to know the information that I needed or
wanted from my wild and restless grandfather. How did he escape
Milledgeville? Was he chased or were the doctors glad to be rid of
him? What was he feeling? What was it like, in the 1940s, along the
river? What did he see? Whom did he encounter? Was he afraid?

Was he, too, transformed?

As I drift along, paddling lazily, I imagine what he would have
looked like swimming with the current, head out of the water, or
shuffling like a bear along the bank, across black roots and blindingly
white sandbars. I want the minutia. But the stories are gone, old stories forever gone.

In subsequent letters I learn that Social Security has made a mis-
take and my grandfather will not have to divorce his wife and leave.
He will not have to putter up the coast toward Brunswick until he
finds good fishing and build himself a shack.

A couple miles downstream we come upon a man and a girl on
a sandbar. Unlikely though it is, they are friends—a writer from
my hometown, Jimmy Johnson, and his high-school-age daughter,
Carrie, who will grow up and go off to the university in Athens and
leave her hometown, which Jimmy has not done. He came home with
a degree.

"Imagine seeing you here," I call to Jimmy.

"Stranger things have happened."

"You're out for the day?"

"Thought we'd do some paddling. Where are y'all headed?"

"Hopefully to the coast."

"We're ready to head back, aren't we, Carrie? We'll ride with you awhile."

"Wonderful."

We pass through Swift Cut with them.

Swift is a new cut that has been slowly making an oxbow. To understand this, we need a short geology lesson: The river is full of bends. Over time the bends deepen and become dramatically U-shaped. Think of someone taking a length of ribbon and tying a bow, making loops. At this juncture of the bow the river does something dramatic. It leaps its banks during freshets and periods of heavy flooding, washes a channel, tearing away trees and vegetation.

Finally one day—usually during winter, with its heavy flooding—the river breaks across the narrow land bridge. The U-curve is now an O. Over time the fresh cut (across the opening of the horseshoe) becomes the main river channel, and the river slowly divorces itself from the oxbow.

As for the oxbow, it functions first as an alternative channel, then as a dead lake, then as a slough. It eventually plugs with sediment and repopulates with willow, cypress, and sweet gum. In this way, the river continually re-creates the swamp forests that it destroys.

A few years ago, when Swift Cut first opened and was still narrow, rapid, and patently dangerous, I helped rescue a boater from it. He was Dr. Presley's grown son, Edwin. It was reunion year, 1999, a Friday, and we were traveling from Gray's Landing to Davis Landing. I was the only woman along, with eight men, eight of the nicest men you could ever meet, although they did not refrain from farting and spitting just because I was a girl.

Edwin was riding as the sole passenger in a canoe overloaded with camping gear, paddling in the stern. He was a fine paddler and had been on the river countless times with his father. He was smart about water and so comfortable with it that he wasn't wearing a life vest.

An overloaded canoe with a single paddler is not an optimal vehicle for a whitewater cut in an alluvial river. For the first few minutes Edwin was fine, alert and paddling hard, but upright.

Let me say a word here about canoes and kayaks. I'm a bit like Mr. Frog in *The Wind in the Willows*. I thought a johnboat was fine until I discovered the canoe. I thought a canoe was grand, superb, an excellent way to travel, until I rode in a kayak.

I have a few friends who are holding out against kayaks, the way I'm holding out against a cell phone. They love the beauty and romance of a canoe, they love the togetherness of one. They will weight the front with river sand and ride in one alone. They are stern about using the correct language of canoes—bow, J-stroke, thwart, rib.

I tell them, "Once you ride in a kayak, you'll never look back."

"We've had this canoe for forty years," they'll say, "and we love it. Why get something else?"

Because a person alone can handle a kayak. It affords independence. It never feels cumbersome, and it responds instantly. A kayak pokes into passages where a canoe can never go. Two people in kayaks can paddle side by side, talking. They can drift side by side, holding hands.

I remember the first time I tested a kayak. I was nervous—the tippiness, the feeling of being trapped by the skirt, the idea of rolling and finding myself upside-down underwater. The boat belonged to my friend Cina, who had been a river guide on the Nantahala and was immersed in river culture. She skirted me up and helped me in. I knew instantly the kayak's power and versatility, and soon I purchased two used flatwater kayaks—no skirt, no rolling.

On the occasion of Edwin's calamity, my kayak came in handy.

I had already made my way through the sluice when Edwin's large and unwieldy boat snagged in a strainer—a river obstacle—in this case, the branches of a downed tree. This can be a very dangerous situation. I was on a downstream bank with a couple of paddlers, surveying others as they rushed through the cut and calling encouragements.

I watched Edwin's boat falter. It tipped and instantly overturned. He went down.

"Man overboard," Charlie hollered.

Edwin's supplies began to float downstream. There went his useless life vest.

Edwin didn't try to fight the water. He miraculously freed himself from the strainer and turned downstream feet-first. In seconds he came to a log he could grasp. There he rested, wondering what to do. He waited.

I saw Edwin make the log.

I also saw the water was too dangerous to be without a life preserver.

"We have to get a vest to him," Crawfish said.

"I think I can do it," I said.

"I have an extra," said Crawfish, who believes in being well outfitted.

This is as good a time as any to say a word about life vests. Most people don't wear them. A long time ago I got in the habit, maybe because I learned to swim as an adult, not as a child, and I never completely trust myself as a swimmer. Let's just say I've never done a triathlon. My rule is not to be caught in a boat, no matter the depth of the water or the brevity of the trip, without a personal flotation device. Living near large, deceptive rivers I have seen more than my share of drownings. Drunk people drown. Sober people get knocked unconscious and drown. Kids drown. I know that people wearing life jackets can also drown, the same as people wearing seat belts die in car accidents, but ninety percent of drownings can be prevented. They're not called life preservers for nothing.

I emptied my boat to liberate weight and cinched my vest tight. I launched carefully and headed upstream.

In the days before fossil fuels, poleboats transported goods to and from the port of Darien. Each side of the boat was equipped with cleated gunnels. A few men positioned themselves along the gunnels, each with a metal-tipped pole stuck in the shallows. To get upstream, they walked backward, leveraging with the pole, pushing the boat forward. Then they dashed forward and repeated this, over and over, singing in unison as they poled slowly and laboriously upriver.

Now the current was so muscular that I couldn't go parallel the bank. The only way to progress was to slice the river at an angle. If I made a far left riverbank, I could portage the canoe and, from the other side of the bend, emerge above Edwin. Propelling upstream, even at an angle, demanded all my energy and concentration. If I rested even a second, I lost many feet I had gained. There was no fiddling. There was no straying of thought. There was no time for a case of nerves.

The song I sang had a two-word refrain: "Left, right, left, right."

My kayak is not as streamlined as most. It looks like a yellow duck— and in fact is called a Mallard—with a narrow bow and a wider prow. It's short and stocky, made for flat water. I keep threatening to trade it in for something sleeker, a kayak that will roll, but I never venture on water that it can't handle. Except maybe Swift Cut.

Around me, the river roared. My friends were yelling but most of what they said I couldn't hear. I assumed they were cheering me on. Downstream, where the cut reentered the main river, others were seining for Edwin's lost possessions, I later learned.

I made the far riverbank, got out, and pulled my yellow boat behind me through the river birch and black willow. I launched again on the far side of the curve and this time paddled only to steer. I didn't want speed. I wanted to slow down. I had to pass close enough to Edwin to get a vest to him. If I missed, or if he missed, I would have to pick up the vest downstream and repeat the entire process.

As I neared Edwin, I lobbed the life vest. It arched in the air, twisted, straps flying, and dove toward the water. Edwin lifted an arm and caught it. He held the log while he strapped on the vest, a feat in itself, then let the water rush him downstream, again feet-first. I landed and repacked my boat. When we reentered the main channel, we regrouped. "Girl, you're a hero," Charlie said. "I want you on my team."

Edwin was ashore. "Thank you," he said.

"You did great," said Dr. Presley. "We thank you."

Friends had salvaged Edwin's waterlogged bags and packages. They had fished his boat from the water and someone was emptying it onshore. We were able to save Edwin and most of what he carried in the boat.

Today, Swift Cut is not the same chute. It has widened, slowed, and become more elderly, clearly the main channel, losing much of its ferocity. It is, however, still full of strainers. The old channel becomes backwater. Even rivers have ghosts.

Jimmy and Carrie take out at Deen's, the landing closest to our hometown of Baxley, Georgia. I was raised on a junkyard my father still runs twelve miles from here, south on US Highway 1. My maternal grandparents' farm, where I spent many adult years, is five miles south.

Deen's Landing is an important landing for Rafthands. It was named for pilot Bill Deen's family. All the time I was growing up, Bill's twin brother, Green, lived with his schoolteacher wife in a house across the highway from the junkyard. He had been a steamboat pilot as well as a cook in World War I. He could make a mean souse, and I still berate myself for not getting his pound cake recipe while he was alive.

After Deen's, the group paddles in a loose affiliation, and all afternoon Raven and I stay out front, heightening our chances of wildlife viewing. Some of us want to rest more than others. Some are more heavily laden. Although we are a group and are watching out for each other, we don't try to stay together, not within eyeshot. Sometimes the first paddlers shore up on a sandbar and wait for the laggards, the ones who have been watching birds and taking dips and collecting flowers. Raven and I feel almost guilty for how lightly we've packed. Crawfish's boat, for one, is stuffed; we offer to carry gear for him and he accepts, handing over a softshell cooler.

We pass beneath US 1, which runs from Maine to Miami. Under this bridge one Easter I hid colored eggs for Silas, a fun-loving little boy who thought that hunting for Easter eggs on a sandbar was as good as being *Tyrannosaurus rex* at Halloween. My nephew Carlin was only a baby.

The bridge has style and class. It was built in the teens, and still (knock on wood) passes the highway inspections. It is almost a mile long. Since I was a girl, my tradition has been to hold my breath as I travel across it, packing lungs with oxygen as I approach, gasping by the time I reach the other side. I still play this game.

One day I'll get too old to hold my breath. One day the bridge will become too old to do its job, and the highway department of Georgia will demand a new bridge. The old bridge then will become a fishing and walking pier, I'm sure, because the people will never let it be destroyed. That bridge is a friend to many.

I have another memory of this bridge. I was here fishing on a date with a local guy, back in my single days. He brought me in his little johnboat. I was having a pleasant-enough time, but my long-term compatibility index with this man was zero. Knowing that, I simply enjoyed the sunlight, fresh air, and an afternoon away from responsibilities. At river's edge, behind one of the bridge abutments, water seeped from a rock face, below which we sat in the johnboat. The cliff was emerald with ferns and moss. I heard a whir and looked up. A ruby-throated hummingbird was hovering beside the cliff wall, catching in its thin beak drops of water as they dripped from an overhanging ledge of moss-soft sandstone.

On a large river, a tiny globe of water was intercepted by a hummingbird.

The bridge marks one of the US Geological Survey's gauges for water level. Streamflow is a measure of a river's width, depth, and velocity, or the volume of water flowing past a point in a given unit of time. Flow rate varies by the minute, hour, day, week, and month, depending on rain events and water releases, as well as by location. The streamflow here this week averages about four thousand cubic feet per second, or about thirty thousand gallons.

Immediately downstream of the bridge, we pass the Edwin I. Hatch Nuclear Plant, built in my home county when I was thirteen or so. I'm not going to say a word about the nuke plant. If I get started, we'll never get down the river. I've got a lot to say about it, but I'm going to wait. I'm going to look the other way, north, and paddle hard to get past it.

I take a peek or two. I see tall, concrete, highly fortified buildings. I see a chain-link fence. I see signs. I see security lights, like there's a baseball diamond up there on the grass. I see a round smokestack, and steam billowing out. I see a taller stack, where radiation gets released.

On the old river maps this area was called Jack's Suck. (I cannot find a definition for "suck" used as a noun in conjunction with a river. I assume the word refers to a whirlpool or crosscurrent that existed here.) Look what happened to Jack's Suck. They built a nuclear plant. Its noise is a constant loud thrumming, humming, buzzing roar. Imagine working eight hours a day in that din. The noise ruins our peace. For a long time downriver we hear it, a different kind of suck.

In minutes we begin to pass alongside Moody Forest, a few thousand acres that have been preserved by The Nature Conservancy and the State of Georgia. I have a lot to say about Moody Forest too. It's the closest wild place to my home, and I've made a lot of walks and seen a lot of wildness back in there.

Early one summer morning, for example, I went into Moody Forest alone to see if an egret roost was a rookery. Bottlebrush was blooming, and the forest floor looked as if a fairy orchestra had just laid down its red trumpets, the flowers of trumpetvine. Squirrels played in the canopy. I heard a deer galloping away. I found the roost but it wasn't a rookery, so I kept going. For a while I stuck to a four-wheeler track, then I began to wander the majestic old forest, thinking of Jake Moody who had loved the place and hoping, to tell the truth, to see his ghost. Or the ghost of my grandfather. I looked at things, animals and ferns and wildflowers and old trees and big trees.

The weather had been very dry, and I was able to walk into places I had only known before as swamp, although the ground was still wet and slurpy with thick, sticky mud. The drought allowed cypress seed to germinate, and the young trees flourished, some a foot tall. Way back in the swamp, sanctum sanctorum, I flushed three wood ducks from what was left of a slough, now a stagnant pool covered with duckweed. In the lime-green skim I noticed two eyes looking at me, an eight-foot gator that retreated uneasily.

I was never once lost. I wanted to go farther.

Another evening I launched my yellow kayak downstream at Morris Landing and paddled upstream, past the forest. I was hungry and filled my mouth with fruit leather, chewing as I paddled, trying not to lose ground; I snatched handfuls of cheese crackers between strokes. I pressed upstream, staying close to the bank. A kingfisher called, then crows. I heard more than one red-shouldered hawk screaming high. Snowy and great egrets waded.

What an abundance of life. I was ecstatic with the beauty of it. Three wild turkeys flew across the wide river in front of me. An osprey circled overhead. Breathing hard, I reached a sandbar on which stood seventeen killdeer and I paddled to one end of it. A gar lay stiff and cold where an angler had tossed it, on sand stained blond, the color of tea. The higher up the sandbar, the lighter the sand. Next to the woods it was white.

Along the Altamaha old-timers remember when the sandbars were much whiter than they are. Now they are polluted with sewage, sediment from erosion, toxins, and algae. In the early 1800s, before the tree-cutting began in earnest, the river was a different river. Its water was stained by tannins from the cypress, which seemed to bleach the sand, not discolor it. Something of the purity of the water can be told by the color of the sandbars.

I dragged my kayak awhile along the bar until I discovered the opening to Rock Creek, but the water was too low to float it. The inlet to Rock Lake was thick with grotesque, awful algae, a sure sign of agricultural pollution. In the shallows were the gaping shells of dead mussels; one remained closed, and when I upended it, water spurted.

I sat at the mouth of the creek and ate a mango, the last of my food. Another osprey flew overhead, dangling a fish beneath, the way some helicopters carry heavy things below their bellies. Then I dragged my boat up into undergrowth, past a big dead flathead catfish, and walked to Rock Lake. Here there was nothing around for miles except the old fat-based, green-leaved tupelo and the cypress with their beautiful knees. A fine backyard.

Maybe it's true of all river stretches, but there's a funny culture along this section. I know it because I've hovered on its periphery. People like to drink out here. These are hardworking men and women, electricians and carpenters, mechanics and welders who labor all week and drink all weekend. They ride leisurely up and down the dirt roads in their trucks, tossing empties out their windows. Sometimes they ride to Morris Landing, where they park and drink. They stay all day. They heap their cans together in piles or try to burn them in their bonfires.

I remember a woman in a white Ford truck flagging me down to ask if I had a cigarette. "I came with three packs last night, and everybody kept burning them," she said. I remember the times the landing was under water for weeks at a time, and the parties relocated to higher ground. I remember one day on the way into Morris Landing coming upon a small truck parked in the dirt road. A man was sitting behind the wheel. The truck's engine was off, and the man was sleeping.

"That's Gage," I said to Silas. His wife had left him for his best friend, Lucky.

"He's sleeping in the middle of the road," Silas said.

"Drunk, I'd say."

"Should we wake him up?"

"No. He might get in an accident if he drives like that. Let him sleep."

Now, on the second day of our voyage to the ocean, we hear an osprey screaming in the sky. She flies repeatedly toward a particular loblolly pine growing tall and lean-topped near the riverbank. Finally she swoops so low she drives a large bird from the tree—a bald eagle! Around us fellow travelers brake against the current, paddling backward, watching to see what will happen. The osprey must be nesting somewhere. The eagle goes flapping off through the swamp.

Our bird list is getting more exciting. An eagle? What does Alaska have on south Georgia except numbers?

For now, I'll say this about Moody Forest. That osprey and that bald eagle are two good reasons why we conserve wild places.

Bird List So Far:
kingfisher, green heron, great blue heron, little blue heron, cardinal, yellow-billed cuckoo, wood thrush, swallow-tailed kite, Carolina chickadee, prothonotary warbler, killdeer, pileated woodpecker, blue jay, common crow, osprey, bald eagle.

Boat by boat we arrive at a sandbar at the entrance to Dead Lake, where Cobb Creek comes in on the "white" side of the river, opposite Moody Forest. The fishing in this spot is supposed to be grand. We will camp here, close to the nuclear plant. Lee, the journalist from Atlanta, unsheathes his fly rod and plies the waters. I brought a rod and reel but have not picked it up, nor do I use it now. Puffs of black willow seed float across the sandbar, like snowflakes or ashes, wind-borne silk, so light they seem unaffected by gravity.

Black willow is synonymous with the upper reaches of this river. It's hard to think of there being one without the other. I've tried to learn about black willow. But, rarely studied, it's a tree with a lot of secrets.

Black willow is *Salix nigra*, native to eastern North America. It's also called white perch willow, for a reason. The bark is dark and deeply fissured. It's a deciduous, fast-growing, frequent-forking, water-loving tree. Viceroy, mourning cloak, and Acadian hairstreak butterflies lay their eggs on it so their larvae can eat its leaves. In spring, black willow sends out golden catkins that produce floating seed, our version of cottonwood.

We watch the slow-motion confetti falling across the hay-colored sand as we begin thinking about supper. When we set up the trip, everybody agreed to bring their own food. However, we have fallen naturally into mutualism, communism. Breakfast and lunch are usually dutch, but each night we pool ingredients and someone cooks for the entire group. Supper tonight is spaghetti with meat, made by Dave, a big man I haven't mentioned before. We contribute vegetables for salad.

I like Dave. He's quiet. He has brought an amazing display of camping geegaws and a prodigious amount of food. He is the one who pulls out folding tables and pounds of sausage. Everything he does is big, the bounty thrilling.

I eat the spaghetti without complaint although I am mostly vegetarian. To be exact, I don't eat industrial meat. I don't ask where this ground beef came from.

We're sitting around postprandial when an insect staggers through camp carrying a spider. It is walking backward.

"What the hell kind of bug is that?" Charlie asks.

Of course Crawfish knows. "It's called a digger wasp. She's going to use that spider to feed her larvae." Somehow he knows it's female.

"You could catch a bream with that."

Crawfish is examining the ground. "Here's her burrow." It's a half-inch hole in the sand, with a piece of leaf for a door.

The wasp abandons the spider occasionally to fly up and scout her whereabouts. She seems to orient herself by the leaf and by a small twig lying nearby. The spider is not dead, only paralyzed. The wasp returns for the spider, drags it backward, then after a time flies up and reorients, amid a bevy of exclamations.

"She'd be screwed if I moved that twig," Charlie says.

"What's really interesting," Crawfish says, beginning anew, "you see that little fly above the wasp?" Sure enough, a miniscule fly is following the wasp like a spy, hovering above her, going where she goes. Crawfish doesn't miss anything. "That fly is watching the wasp. It's going to lay eggs in the wasp burrow. The fly larvae are going to feed on the wasp larvae. Opportunistic, it's called."

"Wow," someone says. There are more exclamations: "Incredible" and "My first thought was that the nuclear plant had created something creepy."

The wasp gains the hole and crams the spider inside. The spy fly disappears into the evening air.

"That deserves a toast," Dave says and fishes out a bottle of wine.

"And a shot of Irish cream," says Crawfish. A cigar is passed and we are laughing around a modest willow-and-driftwood fire. Around us confetti drifts, and soon moonshine flows across our little camp on the sandbar of a great river.

❧   The law had asked us to name our enemies.

"We have none," we had told them.

"Obviously you do."

But who? We flip through mental catalogues of colleagues, trying to ferret out a suspect. Who has poor grammar? Who owns a manual typewriter with pica type? Could someone we know have inadvertently misrepresented us to a more hostile third party?

Have we held an environmental position that angered someone? Are we being targeted for supporting a political candidate? Did my husband's bumper stickers ("MALLWORT: Your Source for Cheap Plastic Crap" or "Grand Oil Party") piss someone off?

The person who owed us a quitclaim deed has now been investigated. The person's typewriter has been examined, and its type does not match the letter. A quitclaim deed is in the mail to us.

For lack of a known enemy, we begin to suspect nearly everybody. Anyone could don gloves, type one line on a sheet of white paper, use a few daubs of water to stamp and seal an envelope (there's DNA in saliva), and then tap out a simple address: Governor Jeb Bush, Florida Capitol, Tallahassee.

Anyone could have misspelled the words "responsible" and "you're." Any crazy could have picked Raven's name out of a telephone book. Bad luck.

That pall is lifting. No phone is ringing. No one is wearing uniforms. No one has a weapon.

Sometimes on long stretches paddling on this second day, we thought about the implications. A threat on the life of a governor is a federal crime, and Raven is afraid of going to jail for something he did not do. He is afraid of the accusation blotting his clean record.

I am afraid of further vengeance. I am afraid of not knowing the enemy, of meeting him or her in a dark alley, not knowing he or she is our enemy. I am afraid of not recognizing the enemy, even if we find out his or her name.

The letter was not a death threat directed at us, so we don't have that dark cloud over our heads. No one is trying to kill us for not being "responsable" people. But he or she, or they, may be trying to put Raven in jail, and at the very least, they are trying to disrupt our lives.

On our second day in a week of days spent gathering armfuls of sun and river, we go to bed without anxiety. If we had known that a second letter had been mailed, we might not have rested.

The Third Day

Early morning we slip past Cobb Creek on the "white" side, then Morris Landing, Davis Landing, and Eason's on the "Indian." All these landings were named for families of early settlers with land holdings in these spots. Clifton, Stripling, Sharp, Kennedy, Hughes.

Morris is undeveloped, sans the pavement that Deen's has, and is the spot where I usually swim with Silas. This is where I come sit on a sandbar and write. If I have three hours to be in a boat, I come here and paddle down to an oxbow, go in, and explore it. Morris Landing has a few small inholdings of private property, where river rats, as they call themselves, jack travel trailers up on pilings. If the floods get higher than their trailers, they mop up the mess, replace the worst of the warped boards, and let her go.

This is the country that Caroline Miller rambled as she collected stories for her book, *Lamb in His Bosom*, which won the Pulitzer Prize in 1934. In 1991, unable to attend a Baxley ceremony held in her honor, Miller wrote an address that was read to the attendees by her nephew, Dr. Ward Pafford. In it she remembers the river: "The Old Altamaha lazes along toward the big water, talking, whispering to itself, its shining surface like crinkled check taffeta on a Sunday morning in May. The dark comes softly down and the ages-old river whispers along its tall shoulders and white sandbars."

At one place that I'll call Buzzard Roost, forty vultures, and easily more, take turns at some bright red mass on a spit of sandbar. Vultures, both black and turkey, roost in the trees all around, some with wings outspread. The easterly flare of sun creeps through cypress branches.

∽ Three of the paddlers are taking out at Eason's Landing, where they've parked a truck. The Rafthands laugh when they remember that the Last Raft couldn't stop at Eason's. Somebody there had promised to kill Bill Deen, should he stop. Bill was known for his love of women.

"I don't cull nobody," he is quoted as saying.

Now, the love feud long over—Mr. Deen in the ground and his nemesis too—we're stopping. Everybody is pretty grimy, and no one really wants to return to civilization, so I elect to go for ice. I take the order and ride on the back of the paddlers' truck to Eason's Grocery, a country store a few miles away. Miz Ann Eason, who runs the store with her husband, Richard, is at the register. They live in the back, like in the old days. I stop in whenever I'm passing, and I try to buy something, to help the store thrive.

Miz Ann has grandkids enrolled at the school my son attended, before he went to Vermont. She always lent us her big popcorn popper for PTO events.

No marketing consultant has ever been able to convince the Easons to take out the wood heater surrounded by chairs, to make room for more shelves. In winter the stove is the heart of the store and of the community. I like hearing the yarns spun there and unfailingly wish I had time to linger. The chairs are empty today.

"Where is everybody?" I ask Miz Ann.

"Probably fishing."

"It's a great day for it," I say.

"Are you all on the water?"

"Paddling a little," I say. "Hoping to get to Darien."

"Just keep going, you'll make it."

"We're needing ice," I say.

"How many?"

"Six." I get everybody a fruitsicle. Miz Ann tells me to be careful, have fun.

Back at the river we sit around and eat our fruitsicles. We are down to a group we christen the Hardcore Heavyweights, eight of us in eight boats. In the days ahead, these are the people I will come to know well. Every person has a reservoir of inexplicable mystery, a façade, a soul in conflict with a personality. Every person is an enigma.

Dr. Presley is one. Crawfish and Charlie make three.

Dave is the fourth. I've already described him, big and steady and self-contained.

Lincoln is the fifth, a thin, quiet man wearing glasses. For most of his life Lincoln worked for the CIA, as a weapons inspector. He's been to Iraq. Definitely he knows many secrets and definitely he knows how to guard them. We keep hoping we can get him drunk enough to tell some really interesting and maybe classified tales. Lincoln is comfortable with technology. He's brought a global positioning system.

Another woman is along. This is Lola, Lincoln's wife, who is calm and pleasant, a slight and handsome woman I associate with golden yellow. She carries her own weight, paddling placidly along in a little bubble of golden-yellow placidity. She and Lincoln love the outdoors but have never paddled for a week before, so everything is new and exciting to them, which makes them even more delightful. They also love each other, a super-relief. Nobody is bickering.

Once, years ago, Raven went down a river with friends on a trip they proudly proclaimed as All Male All Meat. This trip is All Love All Inclusive.

Raven and I, newlyweds, number seven and eight.

Soon after a hearty bye-bye to Eason's Landing, the Ohoopee River pierces the side of the Altamaha.

The Ohoopee is the most beautiful river left in the whole South, I think. It's tiny. Sometimes in the summer it almost dries up, until it becomes only a filament of water through white sand. But it's partly unlogged and mostly undeveloped, and when it carries enough water, it is a stunning passage through floodplain forest, through jade banks of willow that keep the earth cool. Most of its cypress were cut, probably a century ago, but in a place or two, a few mature ones demonstrate what the river used to be and could be again.

The Ohoopee's mouth is unusually shallow, and seen from the Altamaha, it is obscured by black willows marching inward from the banks, closing the river channel. The willows are a curtain. A secret passageway wends through them, leading upstream to a wonderful surprise.

Raven and I don't know it yet—we won't know it for seven years— but we will come to live a mile or two from the Ohoopee, in the triangle, in fact, formed by its intersection with the Altamaha. We have no idea that we'll call it home, will come to know it intimately. We'll fall in love with it.

One day some years ago, motorboating with a scientist and going fast, I witnessed a surreal spectacle at the mouth of the Ohoopee. The time was early in the day, a foggy morning, as river mornings are usually foggy. A clot of people in dark clothes had gathered on the white sandbar. The group was odd-looking, like a caucus of upright buzzards, and seemed to be performing some ancient and sinister ritual. As we neared, I saw it was a group of young canoeists, maybe fourteen or fifteen teenage males all dressed in black. A female counselor whose enterprise seemed to be rehabilitation was talking into a mobile phone at water's edge. I am sure she was wondering how she'd make it wherever she was going with her burden of adolescence.

If I had been alone, I would have stopped. But not everybody is as nosy as I, and our boat swiveled by in a hiss of spray. As we passed, the boys one by one ran up a trail toward the woods, as if back toward something they had found. The sight was strangely disturbing, and it returns to me now as we pass the place—a single-file line running while a counselor huddles into a receiver.

The sandbar is empty now. The Ohoopee pours out its bright load through a filter of willow into the waiting vessel of the Altamaha.

Every place is full of stories. I can't know all of them or tell all the ones I know. One drought-stricken Labor Day my friend Ann Singer, who knows where to find old cemeteries and other wonderful things, and I put in at Carter's Bight and paddled upstream, to the Ohoopee, which was just a trickle. Away from our children (one each) for an afternoon, we were happy, excited to see a green-backed heron and bullfrog tadpoles, then a juvenile white ibis, a bird that wasn't so common on the river ten years ago, before a hotter climate drove more of them north from Florida. (Now sightings of white ibis, wood storks, and even roseate spoonbills are common.)

As happens almost daily in the summer coastal plain, a storm brewed in the sky, a high, dark thunderhead that moved as it assembled. Thunder rambled along the horizon, and in a far corner of the sky lightning flashed. Predicting exactly where storms like this will burst is difficult, but this one appeared to be coming our way. Having seen the dry Ohoopee, we turned downstream, hoping to beat the storm to the landing. It was a large black eye in the sky, staring us down.

Not far to the north the storm was a skyscraper, and when it toppled, somebody was going to get hurt. With each moment the thunder grew louder and louder, and lightning sneaked toward us. Lightning would strike and then thunder would roll, and the time between the two was tightening, until there was no slack. The tempest swept upon us like a cat on keets.

"One thousand one, one thousand two, one thousand three, one thousand four."

"We better get off the water," Ann said as the first drops fell. Her voice sounded as if she were looking over the edge of a high cliff.

"Where?" I asked.

"To the sandbar."

"Like lightning is not going to hit us on the sandbar?" I asked.

"We have a better chance there than on the water," she said.

Lightning struck, close. One thousand one, one thousand two.

"Let's get to the sandbar," I shouted. "Hurry."

We were paddling hard toward land. Rain poured down now and soaked us. The storm's racket was intense.

"Go faster," I hollered.

"I'm going as fast as I can."

"It's getting worse," I said.

We landed our boats, dragged them from the river, and dashed up the beach. "We're going to die," I heard Ann say. I thought she was joking.

"Maybe we should get back in the woods," I yelled.

"The woods?" Ann yelled back. "Lightning hits trees."

"On this sandbar we're the tallest thing around." Rain ran into my eyes, my mouth, down my back.

"I'm not getting around trees," she said.

Miraculously we found a swale on the sandbar, as if in the past some large wind or wave had formed a long mound, with a trough behind it. Bent to the driving rain, Ann and I sprinted for the swale and belly-flopped into it, head to head. Now the thunderhead was directly above us, and close, like a low blue-gray ceiling. Or like getting an MRI while cold and wet, exposed to the elements. I remember lying there in the sand looking up, swiping the rain from my face, trying to get a sense of things, of whether we were safe or not. Suddenly the sky threw a spear of lightning at us, and almost instantaneously came thunder. Zero miles away.

In the next few minutes, the thoughts that came to both of us were ones nobody wants to imagine. We each did some form of praying.

Then the storm took flight as quickly as it had come. Ann and I sat up into new leases on life and a world cleansed by electricity.

⌣ Now, the sandbar at the aperture of the Ohoopee is serene, soporific in May sunshine, edged with the bright-green leaves of spring willow. We pass it by. We overtake Iron Mine Bluff, reputed to be the highest point along the river, owned by friends of my father. I visited the bluff with my folks when Silas was a toddler, my nephew Carlin a babe in arms. It's told that somewhere back up there the KKK used to gather.

Then we pass Carter's Bight ("bight" meaning a long curved section), where Ten Mile Creek pours in. When I lived on my grandmother's farm, Little Ten Mile formed one boundary of the property.

My watershed address was Little Ten Mile Creek @ Ten Mile Creek @ Altamaha River @ Altamaha Sound @ Atlantic Ocean. Ten Mile was so named, according to John Goff in *Placenames of Georgia*, because it was located ten miles via the River Trail west of Old Fort James, a stockade built in 1797 to aid in moving European colonists through Indian lands.

Lower Sister Bluff is veined with iron ore, orange marbling through white sand. Atop it, southern magnolias bloom. Imagine that: white magnolia blossoms on a green canvas suspended above the white sand of a river bluff. Along the riverbank grows coral honeysuckle and royal fern.

Bye-bye, Carter's Bight. Goodbye, Lower Sister Bluff. Got to keep moving, headed on down the line.

Just downstream of Highway 144, Lane's Bridge, at Big Hammock Wildlife Management Area, limestone bears prop scars like the ones on the backs of manatees. More than fifty miles have passed beneath my prow and I have not once mentioned rocks. When I first saw the waters of the north Georgia Appalachians, and then the waters of most other parts of the United States, I was shocked to see them lined and bottomed with rocks and pebbles. Where I am from, the flatlands, the rivers are dug into mud and sand, and far below that, sheets of limestone, visible in occasional outcroppings. We have also a small orange rock, a ferrous oxide, which can be found scattered across the best agricultural land.

But there are no boulders on which to sun. There are no rock cliffs. There are no flat stones to skip. Sand is the record keeper.

We stop because I've been here before, with a mussel scientist, and I know what to find and how to find it. I drag my hands through mud and bring up a mussel, then another.

In a tall tree, three wood storks dry their wings. They take to air with necks outstretched, through a blue sky flowering with white cumulus. Around and around they fly, lazily and elegantly, black stripes on the undersides of their wings.

It's on to Stooping Gum, Beards Creek, Beards Bluff. At Adamson's Fish Camp and Beards Bluff Campground, we stop for supplies and for human company. The establishment consists of a wide-porched general store, bunkhouses, a landing, and a primitive campground. If we were in motorboats, this is where we would gas up.

We rest again on a sandbar a half mile above the maw of Penholloway Creek, and we watch and watch three swallow-tailed kites hunting in the floodplain next to the river. A green leaf floats out of one's talons, proving that their world does touch ours.

Another swallowtail skims the river a half mile past the Penholloway.

In between place-names on a map, there is just water, dark blind water, water without end, bearing us ever onward, seaward, toward some new understanding.

The far coast is a long way away, days, and in long stretches of paddling, when nature is mostly quiet and still—no herds of elephants bugling, no cataracts to navigate, not even a single ferocious alligator—I float along trying not to think. If I think, I try to think about all the beauty around me. And all the good. I try not to worry.

Sometimes to keep my mind occupied, I scribble lists of trivia.

List of the Extraneous Items Fellow Travelers Have Brought:
fold-up table, fold-up chairs, radio, blue lights, matches that strike in the rain, crab meat, plastic egg containers, a muffin toaster (I kid you not), a pineapple, a watermelon, four cell phones, colored pencils, crabber boots, sandwich spreader, shaving cream, battery-operated electric razor, battery-operated fan, nonalcoholic Guinness.

At dusk on the third day, the Hardcore Heavyweights on the All Love All Inclusive Kayak Trip recline in our extraneous chairs on a sandbar somewhere near Old Fort James. We watch five planets line up in the western sky, below a crescent moon. Jupiter is highest, then Saturn, Mars, bright Venus, and Mercury listing above the horizon. All week at sunset the five planets will appear in the sky, tightening their knot. Thursday they will be closest, then they will drift apart again.

"So often we forget that we're part of that universe," Lola says.

"The world is too much with us," Dr. Presley says.

"We once read a study that showed that people who sleep with their heads northward have a better sense of direction," I say.

"What does that have to do with the stars?" asks Charlie.

"We're part of the universe," I say.

The study involves college students given a directional test. The ones who performed worst—meaning those who couldn't find their way around—were housed in dorm rooms in which the heads of the beds pointed north. Six months later, when students were retested, the ones who had been sleeping in the north-pointed beds performed best. At least that's what I remember.

"Anybody up for a little night paddle?" I ask.

"You go ahead," Charlie says. "I've done my day."

"I'm happy to sit right here," says Crawfish. So are the rest.

I'm too fond of sleep to be much of a night naturalist. Tonight I'm energized by the journey and by our surroundings, by the fire and by a universe swirling with stars. Five planets are camped out in the western sky. In darkness Raven and I scratch our kayaks across the beach to the water and turn upstream, hugging the bank. We glide softly, making as little noise as possible. Water drips off our paddles. Far off in the swamp a barred owl poses its ancient questions, and all manner of frog and insect chorus loudly. In the middle of the river, a mullet splashes.

A river at night is magic. The feeling is of weightlessness, of floating not just horizontally but also vertically. Humans own the daylight, animals own night. A night paddle is about breaking biorhythms. It's about becoming animal.

A year earlier, our friend Charlie Ford, who ran a canoe livery, started arranging full-moon night paddles. Raven and I had not been courting long. One July we left the house at 5:30 p.m. for a Moonlight Paddle from Gray's to Deen's Landing. We met at the steakhouse.

We had already eaten—Raven's famous mashed potatoes topped with pan-seared tuna steaks, with steamed asparagus, salad, and bread. (Around the plate's rim he had drizzled blended mango, and at the last minute he ran to the garden for three sprigs of rosemary garnish.) Even so, someone offered a bite of steak to Silas, who never gets his fill of red meat, and soon he was cleaning everybody's plate. Funny what we remember.

The following month we went again. This time Silas stayed with friends. That night I remember in glorious detail. It was a Saturday in August and we planned to paddle from the Uvalda Bridge to Gray's Landing. Raven and I kayaked side by side, through the darkness that precedes the rising of the refulgent moon, while all around us were other vessels, in them friends, invisible arms to catch us should we have capsized.

Soon the moon was an arch being forged at the horizon. As I watched it rise I felt a moth tap against my shoulder, nothing unusual. Another brushed my arm. One fluttered briefly against the back of my neck.

I noticed more and more of them.

"What's with all these moths?" I asked.

"Gosh, you too?" The voice belonged to Bob Brannen, an ardent canoeist from Jesup who would become a river guide.

"They're everywhere," I said.

Moths constantly grazed my face, flew into my hair, alit on my hands.

Charlie flipped on his flashlight and aimed its beam upward. Moths were so thick they were like sparks from a house burning. Someone had called roll and all the nocturnal moths in south Georgia had answered. Along the river hundreds of thousands of them hit the water and lay there, drifting, surrendering to the mouths of fish. We must be out in a hatching, I thought. I had never seen so many, a burden of moths.

No matter what direction Charlie flashed his torch, the air was drenched with moths. They were drawn toward Charlie's beam. They swarmed about us, crazy for whatever the light offered them. Anyone with a moth phobia would have drowned.

The moths were only the beginning. Frogs were hollering wildly, a honking chorus. A strange cry no one could identify rose from the woods.

At the sandbar of Half Moon Round we pulled over to rest. Bob explored the backwater on foot, his flashlight plundering. He called for us to come. In the beam of his light a three-inch toad was calling intermittently. Each time it called its throat bulged purple, although on lengthier inspection we found the vocal sac to be actually a reddish blue, dotted with blackish spots. Maybe it was a Fowler's toad. I wish I could've been sure.

Meanwhile, there was much talk about which moth was smothering us. Someone thought *angel* and someone said it was *ghost*. But neither of those would have been possible, a lepidopterist later told me. I've pored over moth and butterfly books, trying to identify the species by the place and event. To this day I've wondered, wishing I'd fished a specimen from the night water.

Edwin Way Teale in *A Naturalist Buys an Old Farm* writes about two kinds of naturalists. One sort takes interest in the names of living things, making long lists of what they've seen. The other observes. This type wants to know the bird or the fern in its element, in its ecosystem, its niche. I confess that I have been a namer. Maybe it's the poet in me, interested in words. I want to know the *what* more than I want to know the *how*. To remain nameless, to me, is as if to be invisible. As with humans, knowing a name is the first step to understanding a unique character and story.

That night, as we paddled, the moon climbed higher, until the nightscape was almost half as light as day. Without mission, without urgency, with only a membrane of skin between ourselves and the darkened world, we slid through the night, drenched by the moths, tuned to the honks of night birds and the messages of barred owls: "Fish or no fish, it's time to go home."

Wonder is a feeling that is endangered, which puts me in a luckless position, since I am perhaps addicted to it. I get to jonesing for wonder. I have measured my life in its moments, and I have defined the quality of my life by its presence. When it happens, I am.

This evening there are moths, but not the murmurations of them we witnessed that August night a year ago. We turn and sail back. We close the moth door and draw our covers to our chins. I fall asleep and grow wings.

On the night of the third day, eight humans slumber on a south-side sandbar, heads to the north.

The Fourth Day

Sometimes I dream I am eating wild plants. Usually they are growing at the edge of water. I snap off a piece of duck potato to prove to my father that it is edible. I chomp down on it, masticating the leaves, rolling the strange taste around in my mouth. Suddenly I am beset with worry that maybe I was wrong. Maybe it is the white flowers and not the green leaves that are edible. Maybe it is the root.

Sometimes in the dreams I am eating flag iris. Sometimes violets.

～ The dream, I think, speaks to my hunger for wildness. In it, of course, fears present themselves, although fearing a panther or a grizzly bear, I think, is very different from fearing an act of human violence. In my search for relationship with nature, I have attempted to prepare myself for the worst before acting. Sometimes I've had to plow past other people's fear.

I remember one incident. Silas was ten years old, I was a single mom, and I wanted to take him camping. What we needed was a shuttle, or someone to drop us off and pick us up. My brother Dell wished to watch the NASCAR races. My brother Stephen had a fish fry. Roger, my neighbor, had nothing to do, but he kept backing away.

"You mean I can't pay you to follow us to Lane's Bridge, leave the vehicle, then bring us back to Morris Landing with our boats?"

He looked sideways with wild eyes and backed up. I shook my head and went back home.

Silas and I packed a bag of Butterfinger candy bars, a loaf of sourdough French bread, two cans of ravioli, a can of tuna, three nectarines, and three granola bars. We threw in a tent, sleeping bags, and sunscreen.

When Daddy heard what we were doing, he phoned. "Wasn't long ago a farmer was murdered on the river," he said.

I glanced at Silas, who was playing with Matchbox cars. More opposition was the last thing I needed. I walked the phone outside.

"Nobody's gonna murder us," I said.

"A woman alone, with a boy. Someone will see you, follow you, sneak up on you in the night."

"In a motorboat? Sneak?" I asked.

"Go upstream, float down, sneak up on you," he said, as if I were the biggest idiot in the world.

"And then?" I said.

"I don't think you'll recognize a dangerous situation in time to save yourselves."

"You mean I won't shoot someone until it's too late."

"Exactly."

"If I want to go to the river," I said grimly, "I'm going."

"I wouldn't take Silas," he said, "and endanger his life. He can stay here with us."

"My son and I are going camping on a sandbar in the river tonight," I said, slowly and firmly. "That's what I have been saying for fifteen minutes."

"Well, I'm not going to help you," he said.

Silas and I put in at Morris Landing about 4:00 p.m.

Families thronged the beach at the landing, swimming and picnicking. People cast curious glances at our boats, and when we smiled at the people, they smiled back. We hadn't had the boats long: two plastic flatwater kayaks that resembled colorful ducks. I liked the yellow one and Silas liked the turquoise one. In those days in rural Georgia, kayaks were unheard of, and even canoes were few and far between.

Silas had taken to kayaking like sodium to chlorine. I'm proud of that. He will always be able to say he got his first boat when he was ten years old, from his mother.

First, we kayaked upriver. The current, though strong midstream, was weak along the edges. We'd be able to get back easily. We turned and headed downstream. We beached at a sandbar within eyeshot of the landing on the north (Toombs County) side of the river. We swam, then built canals and mountains, topography in the sand. We hadn't settled on this as a campsite, we were just exploring.

I was edgy. Thunderheads built and passed overhead. I hadn't brought a tarp, and the tent leaked. I needed to gather firewood to keep dry for later. Of course, I knew that if it really rained we could always just go home.

Behind the sandbar lay a swamp, and we climbed back in our boats to paddle among the big trees. Ogeechee limes almost ripe hung like green thumbs from huge, fat-based tupelo. From the winter flood the bases of trees were covered with a dried green moss clumped like scouring pads around the roots.

Silas in his little boat began to explore, squeezing through moss-cushioned trunks of trees. Natural foam in the swamp water flecked the boats.

"Don't you love this," he said.

"I do," I said.

After a while we came back out to the river. I'd seen what looked like a good place to camp, on the south side. "Let's go explore that other sandbar," I said.

"Not yet," Silas said.

I followed his lead as he paddled across the river and back to the north side. He seemed comfortable now.

Late afternoon, as we approached the sandbar I'd scoped out, a dozen wild turkeys fled. They had been foraging in a patch of ripe grass between the sandflat and the woods. The sandbar was inaccessible to full-size vehicles, cut off by a small creek, although I saw that four-wheelers had been crossing.

We erased wild turkey tracks as we set up camp on an embankment ten feet high, underneath a willow, beside a sycamore, with nothing to mar our view. Our tent faced east, toward a little fire we had built.

Silas pulled his kayak atop the embankment, got in it, and pushed off. Using his boat as a sled, he entered the water at a glide, otterlike.

At dusk a full moon rose from the floodplain.

We launched our boats again in darkness and glided out across the face of the water. The moon lifted like an orange balloon through the river swamp, that fast. The sky was lighter and lighter, cloud-stands strewn, skeins scattered.

We yelled up the eddy creek, *Hello! Hello*, called the swamp after a pause. *Moon! Moon*. Swamps echo like the sides of mountains. They return everything you say. *Porcupine, porcupine. Good night, good night*.

At sunrise the world was multicolored. But mostly purple. Fog shrouded the riverbank, where four great egrets hunted. A couple of killdeer announced morning.

"Isn't this so pretty here?" Silas said now. "Isn't it just plain beautiful?"

I didn't know what to say. I could have agreed. Yes, it's pretty. It's just plain beautiful. Instead, I sat in my kayak like a peaceful Buddha, beaming on the universe, which is all good.

After a while I formulated an observation possibly worthwhile.

"I can see almost every color from here," I said. "There's yellow, a tiger swallowtail. Orange—a monarch flew by your head."

"Green trees, blue water," Silas joined in. A kingfisher called.

"Purple in the sky."

"White from the egrets."

"And red!" I pointed to a few red leaves.

When I looked again, Silas was standing in his kayak, trying to pee. "No," he said suddenly, abandoning his zipper. "I don't want to play the Dancing Fool." He climbed out to a woods-meadow, thick with grass.

Later he tried standing on the prow of his boat. He lost balance and fell into the shallow, darkwater creek. He climbed back up, only to lose balance and splash again.

Thus the morning passed.

I realized that for the entire time we camped, from afternoon to morning, we saw not one person, not since the last johnboat had passed toward the landing, the two fishermen in it waving. Nobody.

The whole time it had been only a human mother and a human boy, playing fearlessly among the wild animals at the river.

꩜ On the fourth day, paddling is easy and we see our first alligator, a small one, less than four feet long, that quickly sinks. We camp at Marrowbone Round, where Tom's Creek enters. Crawfish says that twenty years ago this section was a cut, but now it's the river, leaving Marrowbone Round a backwater. Tonight Dave makes chicken and rice, warm, filling, and delicious.

Tom's Creek is a heron rookery. All evening, yellow-crowned night herons overhead make strange flapping and brushing movements in the dark. The breeding plumage of the large gray and yellow birds whispers against the draping leaves of willow. In some of the slipshod nests, hens incubate teal-blue eggs, and in others, gawky, big-eyed chicks doze in the darkness. A strange fog swirls about. We sit around a fire on the sandbar.

"At least the mosquitoes only come out dawn and dusk," Raven says.

"Crepuscular mosquitoes," I say.

"Purgatory mosquitoes," says Charlie.

A geometry of white ibis flies overhead, away from the sunset. "A crepuscular V of ibis," I say aloud.

"This is a pleasant life," says Dave.

"Just hanging out in a beautiful place with wonderful people," says Crawfish.

"Don't forget the beer," says Charlie.

The days are pleasant and the evenings more so. There is so much to see and talk about and think about, none of it stressful.

I'm the first to get tired and I sneak off to bed early. I lie in the dark, watching the flickering firelight on the walls of the tent. I am close enough to hear some of the talk, and I lie on the dark bosom of the earth, listening to my earth friends.

Lines Heard around the Campfire:
"She really has married a barbarian."
"How many countries are there in the world?"
"You could be planning your tee-off time, instead of fighting mosquitoes out here."
"When I got to the ground, I said, 'That's my first and last time.'"
"I had never been rappelling before."
"Tomorrow's supposed to be real nice."

The Fifth Day

In the morning we determine that what looked like fog the night before is smoke. As the morning comes on, the smoke thickens. With
the heat and humidity, smoke makes the river look primeval, as if we
are floating in a world before recorded time. We come upon a fisher-
man checking his trot lines, hooked cords that get baited and tied to
tree limbs at water's edge and then checked periodically. The man is
amazed by our flotilla.

"How many of y'all is there?" he asks.

"Eight," Dr. Presley says.

"A small army."

We laugh.

"Say, where is the smoke coming from?" Dr. Presley asks.

"Okefenokee is burning," the man says.

"Okefenokee?" I say to Raven. "That's a hundred miles away."

"We're breathing Okefenokee carbon," says Charlie.

"It reminds me how interconnected we are," says Crawfish.

"How implicated," I say.

"How insignificant," says Raven.

We leave Marrowbone Round. Through the Okefenokee haze, an
osprey stares down from a snag at the edge of cutover land.

Hughes Landing, Oglethorpe Bluff, Oglethorpe Reach. According
to folklore, General James Edward Oglethorpe, who arrived at what
is now Savannah in 1733 and for the next decade settled the land between the Savannah and Altamaha rivers for England, trespassed on
Creek lands and found himself under attack. He saved himself by
jumping off a high bluff north of Jesup, which forever bears his name.
Historian John Goff, however, calls the story "far-fetched," saying

that no documents prove that Oglethorpe ever visited the area, although he could have.

Hughes Old River, Goose Creek, Linden Bluff, Buggs Bluff, Buggs Suck.

Even at the current's pace, we are moving so quickly that to know these places is impossible. They are simply place-names on maps, fleeting visions of cypress and magnolia, the click-clacking of a rain crow or the hilarity of pileated woodpeckers. At each bluff, each bar, each creek, I want to stop and explore, fashion myself a palmetto shanty and stay awhile.

The eight of us are a community now. For parts of the past couple of days we have tied up together and rafted as a single unit. On one of these party rafts, during happy hour, Charlie shared his theory that beer is the root of human civilization.

"More aptly the downfall of civilization," I say.

"No really," Charlie says. "Bread was invented to store grain to start beer."

"Then we were doomed before we even got started," Lincoln says.

"And not only human civilization," says Crawfish, and he tells about a time he saw a flock of drunk robins.

"Maybe all civilizations are doomed," Raven says.

List of Alcohol Along:
moonshine, tequila, Irish cream liqueur, rum, chardonnay, merlot, Foster's, Tecate, Beck's, Corona, Heineken, Natural Ice, Coors Light, Busch, nonalcoholic Guinness (it has about half a percent).

Lincoln determines with his global positioning gadget that when we are rafted together, we travel 1.5 miles an hour in the current. If we drift over to the edge, as a mass, we slow considerably, less than a mile an hour. Separate, we go somewhat faster than 1.5. I read somewhere that the speed of drift in the Altamaha is about four miles per hour, and maybe it is, in extreme flood, but we have newfangled equipment that says 1.5, which is still a good clip.

According to the global positioning satellite device, then, we can go a mile and a half in an hour. We have seventy-five miles ahead of us. That's fifty hours, a week's work plus overtime.

Nobody cares how fast we go. We have all week. We have time to bunch up. Nobody wants to go home, certainly not us. As far as Raven and I are concerned, we can reach the ocean and turn north.

"Who wants to stop at the Bite and Tickle shop?" asks Charlie.

We all do. Pat's Bait and Tackle serves the Jaycee Landing near Jesup, Georgia, just above Doctortown. There we buy candy bars and more beer. Somebody picks up a Savannah newspaper, and sure enough, there's a story about the Okefenokee fire, but little information on how extensive it is or what parts are burning. At the pay phone Raven and I telephone our friend Jackie, who lives on the edge, and no one answers. We leave more messages for Silas.

When I pick up the front section of the paper, my jaw drops. A picture of me is there. I lower the newsprint, look around, then pick it up again. I'm wearing lipstick, smiling. I don't look like a criminal, a fugitive. "Writer to give talk in Savannah," the headline reads. That reading in a few days is the farthest thing from my mind. To be so far out of regular society, only to find myself squarely in it, is a weird shock, and I feel as if I can't escape my life as an author, or as if I am split—one of me is private, on a river, far from the public, and the other of me is squarely in what is. I am in the world. I am in the good and the bad no matter what.

"Look at this, guys," I say.

Charlie hoots: "You look nothing like your picture," he says. My hair hasn't been brushed in five days, and my clothes are increasingly gray blue.

"That must be a strange feeling," Crawfish says.

"It is."

I am a fugitive, of course. I'm a fugitive from vendettas, from societal dysfunction, from evil and corruption, from money-grubbing, from industrial control of our lives, from disabled landscapes.

Nobody can run forever, the newspaper proves, or even for long.

A quarter mile farther, alas, we run past the timber company Rayonier's paper mill, huge with its white towers and ramps and buildings, its rows of holding ponds, and then we hit the efflu-ent. A red plume trails from an outflow pipe, turning the river a strange briny color. The air has the weird and awful smell of rotten eggs.

In February 2009 a group of paddlers from southern Florida and Wisconsin will spend a week on the Altamaha. They too will stop at Jaycee Landing. One of them will write an account of the trip, pub-lished anonymously online. "As we are eating our lunch the wind brought upon us a very nasty acrid and chemical smell. It was from the local paper mill. As we paddled past the mill we found that the water also contained the same awful smell because the plant dumps into the Altamaha. The smell followed us for two days down the river. This was the only negative part of our trip."

A river is not a trash can, not a sewer, not a dump. How could a corporation be allowed to do this?

Easily, unfortunately.

The stinking paper mill ruins the history of Doctortown, a vil-lage named for a native chief called Alleck, a name derived from the Muscogee word alecha, meaning "medicine man" or "root doctor." A surveying party in 1768 called the site Doctors Town, and contempo-rary Alex Creek testifies to Chief Alleck's memory.

With the infusion of steamboats for navigation, Doctortown boomed. Stagecoaches changed teams here. A sawmill was built. In 1857 the Savannah, Albany and Gulf Railroad Company built a 100-foot-wide railroad trestle across the river, which became the white man's north-south trade route. Before a decade was out, the trestle would become the scene of a bloody Civil War battle.

By December 16, 1864, Major General William Tecumseh Sherman's March to the Sea was well under way. He ordered the railroad bridge at Doctortown destroyed, to prevent its being used by Confederate troops. The Confederates rallied to save the trestle, which was useful in evacuating troops and civilians, and grouped on the south side of the river. They set up two cannons on the bluff there and mounted a third cannon on a flatcar pushed by a locomotive.

On December 18 the battle began. All day men fought, were wounded, and died, so many that it is said that the river ran black, the blood of Northerners and Southerners mingling in the dark streaming water. Whether this happened or not, I don't know. This is a common description of the aftermath of battles. (A woman almost one hundred years old told me she heard that after an Indian massacre on Slaughter Creek in Tattnall County, the creek ran red with blood.) At dusk in the Battle of Doctortown, Northern troops, seeing they could not take the trestle, withdrew and returned to Savannah.

Around us, nothing would indicate a battle. The trestle stretches rusty across the river above us, and perhaps if we climbed it, we could find the marks of shot and bullet. All we have left to know what happened are the stories that were passed down, on paper or orally, memory to memory. Every moment vanishes from itself. Even landmark events fade into the ceaseless stream of the past.

We have no proof of anything.

I say we have no proof, but once I explored a paddle-wheel boat that was partially sunk here, while a swallow-tailed kite sailed overhead. I found a supersized iron crescent wrench, over three feet long, a tool from the wreck. That's some kind of proof.

◡ I have been describing the swamps that insulate the river, but I have not talked about what I know lies on the yonder side of the swamps. The gallant pine forests that once populated the river basin have been cut to death, and the wider corridor of the river, beyond the floodplain, is a landscape of clear-cuts and planted pine fields. Most of the upland forests in this place have been razed.

To me, this is another kind of evil. Before I upset anybody, I will explain. Humans need trees. In the industrial age they have become particularly useful. We are reliant on the paper that comes from their boughs, for one thing, and on the wood ripped from their boles. I am not opposed to tree cutting.

I am opposed to industrial tree cutting that is unregulated and that is happening on a scale so titanic that the damage is irreversible. I'm opposed to taking everything. I'm opposed to clear-cuts because they are the products of capitalism at its worst and greed at its best. Small minds think clear-cuts.

Ecological foresters, including Leon Neel of Thomasville, Georgia, have developed tree-harvesting systems that do not destroy the forests themselves. Sustained yield, Leon calls it. These are selective cuts—the trees to be cut are chosen based on disease, spacing, presence of wildlife, prior damage, and shape. "We never cut the entire forest," Leon says. "We cut individual trees."

Leon once told me about a property in Thomas County that he managed for fifty years. On this property, a timber cruise in 1941 counted 25 million board feet of timber. Over the years, with an annual cut, 46 million board feet of timber have been harvested. Even so, when the property was last cruised in 1995, it still contained 63 million board feet of timber, and it supports the highest population of red-cockaded woodpeckers on private land anywhere.

I'll crunch the numbers. Eighty-four million board feet of timber grew in fifty-four years. Forty-six million were logged. Sixty-three million are left for the woodpeckers, sparrows, bobcats, fox squirrels, bluebirds, tree frogs, and gnatcatchers. Sixty-three million are left for the owners to enjoy. This is their investment in the future, better than the stock market, better than bonds, better than a bank account in the Cayman Islands.

"It takes fifty years to grow a fifty-year-old tree," Leon says. "It takes one hundred years to grow a hundred-year-old tree. Some people forget that. It takes several generations to restore a forest."

Past Knee Buckle Island, Shoe Island, Cole Eddy, and Dog Eddy, the plume and the stench of the paper mill follow us. Nobody is swimming now. Nobody is trailing hands in the water. Nobody even wants the paddles to drip on them.

Powderblue damselfly
drifts on a stick
in the contaminated water.

"Wonder how this place got its name?" Charlie asks when we reach Yankee Round midmorning.

"Could the Northern troops have camped here?" Dr. Presley asks, in true Socratic fashion.

"That's what I'd surmise," says Dave.

Some of us aren't native southerners, my husband included, and we start talking about the differences between the North and the South. The North is too cold, the South too hot. Northerners are more efficient. Southerners are friendlier. Northerners drink tea plain, southerners sweeten it. Northerners eat cream of wheat, southerners eat grits. Southerners are too fat, northerners too skinny.

"Let's declare the war officially over," I say. "We'll make a new country, the United States of the South!"

"Come over and kiss this Yankee," Raven says.

When I do, we almost upset and tip ourselves into the nasty river.

About midday we see five Mississippi kites in a tree. In a tree! I've never seen one not airborne. A Mississippi kite is a close cousin of the swallow-tailed in beauty. They are darkly elegant, a lighter gray with a lustrous suedelike texture. They have extraordinary grace and agility, due in part to an average wingspan of three feet, and make quick aerial maneuvers, snatching insects from the air. The kites are an uncommon and glorious sight.

Only its forked tail makes the swallow-tailed kite more fleet and lovely.

We stop for lunch under a flank of shady willows and watch a pocketbook mussel scribing a looping line through hot, shallow edgewater toward the bank. The mussel siphons water in and out. We wade close and gaze through John's macrobinoculars at its ivory folds of soft skin, almost sexual. The mussel leaves a very visible track in the submerged sand. Above us, a swamp ash hangs with samaras. Pishing, we attract a blue-gray gnatcatcher. Everything we see strengthens my fealty to the place.

One New Year's Day I hiked with Neill Herring and other Jesup friends to a piece of timberland somewhere near here. I remember having a really good time. We were celebrating Neill's daughter Helena's sixteenth birthday, and I remember us swinging on vines in the floodplain. I remember a huge cypress. I remember thinking that all over the country, families and friends were celebrating the new year with a big meal and a walk. But not many of them were walking in a swamp.

Lake Bluff, Doe-head Eddy.

At evening we camp on the Indian side of the river, across from Hannah's Island, thought to be haunted. After supper a couple of us kayak across to the island. Hogs have been raking the forest floor, trying to sweep up the fallen blooms of trumpet vine. Lizardtail droops its long bloom near a stand of river cane. Poison ivy grows lush. We wander upon a single spider lily in bloom. We explore farther into the swamp: thirty minutes later, returning, we tread near the spider lily: a second bloom has opened.

More Birds:
red-shouldered hawk, spotted sandpiper, Mississippi kite,
prothonotary warbler, great egret, snowy egret, cattle egret,
bank swallow, barn swallow, mourning dove, anhinga, white ibis,
turkey buzzard, barred owl, yellow-throated warbler, nighthawk,
wood duck, purple martin, summer tanager, fish crow, red-bellied
woodpecker, indigo bunting, yellow-crowned night heron, parula
warbler, red-tailed hawk, ruby-throated hummingbird, black vulture,
mockingbird, great-crested flycatcher, swallow-tailed kite, chimney
swift, ring-billed gull, common grackle, blue-gray gnatcatcher, least
tern, cormorant, rufous-sided towhee, wood stork, chuck's-will's-
widow, red-winged blackbird, laughing gull, rock dove, boat-tailed
grackle, ring-necked dove, brown-headed cowbird, clapper rail.

That night, around our campfire, Dr. Presley tells the story of the ghost of Hannah's Island.

I've encountered a few versions of this story. Sometimes Hannah is a whore. Sometimes the men are soldiers, sometimes rafthands. The men "have her." They "know her." None of the versions, except mine, uses the word "rape." Sometimes the men, in their guilt, kill her.

> A young woman lived with her folks in the vicinity of Doctortown. Her folks were called away to visit a relative who was deathly ill, and the woman was left alone to take care of the homestead. She was visited by a group of rafthands, raped by a skulk of men, a brutality that led to her death. Hannah is not forgotten, and Hannah does not forget, but wanders the swamp of her home, seeking either revenge or peace.

I despise stories of brutality, true or not. They confuse us to our purpose on Earth, which is to be stewards of the mysteries of God. A swamp is God's country. It is full of mysteries, from the one-toed amphiuma to moths that glow in the dark, from the vine that exhibits a cross when dissected, to bright warblers passing overhead on voyages north and south. A swamp is no place for violence. A swamp loves.

And a swamp forgives, which is one reason I am in it.

In the night, on a sandbar about three miles beyond the paper mill, barred owls call back and forth, filling the river swamp with their strange haunting ululations, tracing the mournful ghost of Hannah in her sojourns through a dark wood, in her rising above malevolence.

The Sixth Day

At sunrise strings of ibis fly over, just as a sliver of golden moon ascends in the east above Hannah's Island. We eat our breakfasts without stoking the fire, and by 9:00 a.m. we are on the water again. Around Mile 84, we enter the Narrows, a stretch where the river shrinks and the curves are tight, as if the waterway is kinked. This is said to be the most scenic portion of the river. The current is faster, so we don't have to work hard, simply keep our bows in the current. Most of the day we are shaded by the overhanging canopy, with little more to do than listen to birds—parula and prothonotary warblers, yellow-bellied sapsuckers and downy woodpeckers.

I have a poor photocopy of a historic map of the river drawn by one S. Cooper in October of 1888 and submitted by his superior, O. M. Carter, to the US Engineer Office in Savannah, Georgia, on June 12, 1890. The map is carefully lettered with old names of places along the stretch where we now ride. He marks "Beginning of Narrows" and "End of Narrows." Double Yellow Bluff, First Water Oak Round, Johnson's Bluff, Second Water Oak Round, Steamboat Cut, Harmon's Bluff, Webb's Stump Bight, Bax Point.

In the days of serious water navigation, almost every turn of the river had a name given to it by antebellum poleboaters and by early rafters. Jack's Suck, Tar Landing, Kneebuckle Bend, Mad Dog Island, Devil's Elbow. "Many a raft has broken up at Devil's Elbow," wrote Brainard Cheney, author of *River Rogue* and *Lightwood*.

Some of the names are with us permanently, some are lost.

Soon after Bax Point I watch Charlie, sitting handsome and broad-shouldered in his hand-built kayak, haul himself over to a willow tree and step out on land. I pleasure in Charlie's company. He deeply enjoys life. He draws out a long pocketknife and plunges it through his shirt, then rips off the hem, unwrapping it from around his body as he pulls.

He swivels to a drooping willow and hangs the long, red strip on the tree.

I have reached him. "What in Sam Hill are you doing?"

"Got to treat the willows," he says.

Rag Round, or Rag Point, is legendary. Back in the rafting days, when the rafters passed it they tied an item of clothing or a strip of cloth to a tree for good luck, until the point looked like a bunch of Christmas trees. Or an arboreal clothesline. A bloom of rags. Bad things happened to rafters who did not sacrifice clothing here. Legend has it that one boy was instructed to rid himself of an item of clothing as he passed the point. But the poor boy had nothing that he could afford to give away. The boy never made it to Darien, killed in a log sweep along the way.

One after the other, we pull up next to the willows and tie rags to them. I give up my bandanna.

We're at ninety-five river miles, which means forty-two to go.

Midmorning we stop on a sandbar that has a cold fresh spring running behind it, where we rinse our clothes and take a dip, our first submersion since Rayonier's paper mill. This is Penholloway Creek (spelled Phinholloway on the old map), and here the Narrows end.

Old Hell Bight, Sister Pine Round, Bryant's Wood Yard, Miller's Lake, Obery Sand Bar, Ellis Creek, Upper Sansavilla Bluff.

That evening camped below Lower Sansavilla Bluff, Raven and I decide to swim across the river. When I was a child, doing so seemed impossible, the river unbelievably wide. Besides, I couldn't swim. I heard stories of my grandfather and other terrifically strong men swimming it. In fact, the river set some men apart, as in *He stomped on his hat, then jumped in and swam the river for fun*. For weaklings like me, Lower Sansavilla Bluff, where the river is narrower, is the place to cross.

Raven and I stand a moment in the shallows, as if preparing a baptism. We won't be able to go straight across, toward a lone river birch, but will be swept at an angle with the current.

"So look downstream," Raven says. "Try to land at that cypress stump."

"I'll aim for it," I say.

"Aim for the birch," he says, "and you'll end up at the stump."

"I'll try."

For most of the width of the river, the current is mild, and swimming is simply a matter of concentrating on the breath (to the right, to the left) while pulling handfuls of water past me, hand over hand. I extend my legs to harness their full power and kick like a pair of scissors. Tired of overhand, I sidestroke awhile. Now the bank ahead is closer than the one we left behind. I sidestroke on the other side, pulling hard. The river is manageable until we are twenty feet from shore, where the current turns sharp. We overshoot the stump by ten feet and climb out across cypress roots.

"You did it," Raven says.

I gasp for air. "Yes," I say. Any triumph I feel is eclipsed by self-doubt. "Now we just have to get back."

"You swam great," he says. "Just remember to let the river do most of the work."

I get up.

"Rest awhile," Raven says. "Regain your strength. You did great."

We walk upstream, going farther up so that we can come out near our friends. Below our encampment the river makes a sharp curve, and a tall, brief bluff rises. Getting out there would be impossible.

"If we don't make the sandbar, float past the bluff and head down to that marshy area."

"Where the brown grass is?"

"Right there. Ready?"

"Ready."

We ease into the water. The return is much harder because the swift current must be traversed first and because I am excited and tired. The water is deep, over our heads. We know from swimming near camp that it drops off eight feet from the long sand bank, and here it must be twice that deep. I have to keep a tight rein on my panic. Raven stays beside me, his gaze rarely leaving my face. I don't look at him, because I am not going to think he can save me. I am thinking of myself, that I am strong, I can swim this river. I will not drown. I try to relax, as much as a person can relax in the middle of a river that seems bottomless and endless.

I am sure I'll miss the sandbar. I begin to think that I will miss the bluff too and have to overshoot, to the shallow marsh. On shore everybody is watching.

Their concern gives me strength. The last twenty feet, I battle the current. Even when I am a couple yards from land, the fight isn't over, the river grabbing, claiming, gouging. I struggle out of its arms and beach ahead of the bluff, Raven right behind me. From the sandbar upstream I hear cheering.

I sit awhile, breathing hard. *Me and you, river.*

At camp our six friends are full of congratulations. On the sandbar Charlie stir-fries vegetables—golden beet, celery root, potato, sweet potato, parsnip, turnip, tomatoes. He sprinkles on creole seasonings, salt, and pepper, and serves the mixture over wild rice. He's a hell of a cook. As we eat we sit talking about givers and takers.

In general, I'm not much of a team player. I have a dark streak of individualism. I prefer solitude to bad company, and sometimes even to good company, meaning I like great company and I like myself, but not much in between. I have tried group wilderness experiences, and as much as I hate to admit it, I'm not cut out for them. Once I was on a week-long wilderness hike with friends. We adopted the Communist manifesto, "from each according to his or her ability, to each according to his or her need." Honestly, the Communist credo doesn't really work for me. If I haul fifty pounds all day on my back, I don't necessarily want to share my organic, ginger-studded, dark-chocolate bar with the person who hauls thirty. I recognize my resis-tance as a weakness, a selfishness; communal living is for the more highly evolved, which I am not. I have tried to change.

Further, meetings are difficult for me. I have often found that to do something alone goes more quickly and more efficiently than enlisting help from others. That's probably why I'm a writer instead of an organizer.

This trip is working well because I can choose how much I interact and how much I drift apart. I have my own boat and I can paddle when I'm energetic, float when I'm tired. Nobody calls a meeting.

Generosity, oddly enough, may be the major contributing factor for my independent streak. The tendency to take care of others before taking care of myself sometimes forces me into solitude. I can't not be generous. I share, even when I shouldn't.

Supper tonight is a medley of contributions. That we all benefit from sharing suppers is plain to see. We're not all having to cook every night, plus we get to enjoy the marvelous culinary skills of others.

Lincoln and Lola go off to bed, and night comes fully. Raven and I sit side by side, watching John and Dave and Charlie make preparations for night. We are within the constant lull of the river, a willow tree whispers above us. In the willow, an anole pops his moneybag in and out. The sand is cool.

"What do you think happens to a soul when a person dies?" I ask Raven.

"I don't know," he says.

"Do you think there's a hell?" I press.

"No."

"What about heaven?"

"Heaven," Raven says. "I think there's a heaven. I'm already in it."

The Seventh Day

We leave the sandbar beach near Lower Sansavilla Bluff at 8:55 a.m., early for us, because we want to hit the tide. High tide will be at 9:30 a.m. in Darien. We paddle for an hour against the tide, then through the calm turgidity of high tide, until the waters turn and bear us coastward. The paddling is effortless. We arrive at Everett City about noon. Everett City is a small encampment of trailers and campsites centered on a store and a landing. At the pay phone I leave messages for Silas. Raven and I share a pint of butter pecan ice cream.

At the landing we happen into two friends, Christi Lambert and Alison McGee of The Nature Conservancy. Christi, of course, very capably directs the Bioreserve Project, and Alison, tall and willowy, an ecologist by training, heads up conservation. They are conducting a tour of the river for a Georgia leadership group, and have stopped for lunch under a pavilion, in a cloud of bug repellent they hope will spook the yellow flies, horse flies, sand fleas, and mosquitoes. The leadership group is made of people who hold public office in the state. They are dressed more officiously than we. They are cleaner. Christi asks our group to come over and speak a few words to her group, and we oblige. Dr. Presley explains to them what we are doing.

Someone wants our autographs on a scrap of cardboard.

The public world, with its offices and air conditioners, its white shirts and heels, its books and telephones, is a world away from this riverbank, out of which grow alligator flag, marsh grass, and cattails.

We're out of beer, and the fish camp doesn't sell it. Charlie is determined to acquire some. He finds a sympathetic guy who'll drive him three miles out to a store. When he gets there, the store doesn't accept credit cards, so he has to borrow thirty-three dollars from the man who gave him a lift. When Charlie gets back, we round up the money to pay the man. This is what the old rafthands would have done. If they camped near a settlement, they would have sent someone up the hill to trade for fresh food or liquor. They would have passed the hat among the crew.

We set out again and soon turn left and paddle through the beautifully surreal, new-green-of-cypress, wonderfully named Alligator Congress. The whimsicality of black willows is behind us.

I love all the river, but my favorite part, despite the bugs, is the delta, which we are entering. At first a paddler encounters upland live oak and Sabal palm wonderlands interspersed with tidewater swamps where red bay and swamp palm become understories of cypress, sweet gum, tupelo, and swamp black gum. The trees lean out over the water. Swamp mallow, clematis, and wild potato bloom streamside. Tides along the Georgia coast rise as much as seven to nine feet at times, and their influence extends forty miles inland.

This territory is a herpetologist's dream world: mud snakes, rainbow snakes, red-bellied water snakes, yellow-bellied turtles, Florida cooters, alligators, cottonmouths. Grey squirrels dash among the branches; deer, feral pigs, and raccoons leave evidence of their presence in black mud.

All afternoon we face a strong headwind. Paddling is rough, and I wish for a more streamlined boat and a feathered paddle. Often we hug the black-mud bank, which is veined with muddy roots exposed by outgoing tide. Armies of fiddler crabs retreat like fearful waves across mudflats. "Oh, no, the humans are coming!" Raven squeaks, giving voice to the crabs in Gary Larson fashion.

Patches of giant cutgrass, mixed with wild rice, pickerel weed, and arum, begin to occur, then extensive saltmarsh flats of spartina and needlerush, parting for sea ox-eye and sea lavender. Seaside sparrows, clapper rails, and marsh wrens sing from the rushes.

In the delta the river divides into many braids, all leading to the coast—the Darien, Butler, Champney, and Altamaha rivers—weaving through an archipelago. These islands are jungly high ground amid tidewater delta and floodplain, not the typical beach-and-surf islands.

We have a small debate among ourselves—should we take Rifle Cut? This is a mile-long ditch that shoots through the floodplain at a sweeping curve in the river. Enslaved black workers were forced to dig the cut in the 1820s, planters having the idea that the river would soon overtake and claim the "swift," abandoning its main channel and cutting off four to five miles of sandbars and meander, particularly Couper Bar, which was treacherously shallow at low tide. That never happened. Rifle Cut is still a narrow passage through Sabal palm and live oak, a yardstick of efficiency at which the river continues to laugh.

"Let's follow the original course," says Dr. Presley, and that's that. All agree.

By midafternoon we enter Studhorse Creek. From Studhorse we turn up Lewis Creek, which leads past Lewis Island. It is deep and wild, its vegetation lush and junglelike. Clumps of royal fern grow six feet across. Otters, minks, and muskrats live in the wild luscious creek. A spider floats belly up.

On the 5,600-acre island are cypress over a millennium old, which means their germination dates before 1000 CE. Some of them measure over seventeen feet in diameter, and every year they grow older and larger. One is said to be 1,300 years old. The island was logged prior to 1920 save for forty to fifty acres that escaped the logger's saw. Nobody knows why. Myth has it that the stand was out of cable's reach, but waterways run fairly close by. I like to think loggers spared these trees not because the trees were too far removed or their girth too broad for the saws, but because they were spiritually too big to touch. They are God.

Once I hiked in at low tide, the only time a person can get in, to see the cypress, following orange marking string for a hard half-mile slog through knee-deep mud. I was barefoot, banging my feet on cypress knees—the mud sucks off any kind of shoe that isn't tied on, and all I'd brought was sandals. But I found the old cypress, trees so old they seemed to have become ethereal in the way of very old people. Flag iris were blooming among the living musical towers.

Not enough can be said about the floodplain forests of the delta and swamps in general. They are a naturalist's heaven.

Cypress and tupelo create a vast tree cave, a dim movie set. The trees grow thick and stout, their trunks buttressed. Here, a red maple sprouts from a crevice in a cypress. White ibis, great egret, and little blue heron wade in shallows. A solitary sandpiper looks for something she lost along the creek's edge. The tail of a snake disappears into a hollow tupelo. A beautiful, tiny tree frog with peach and green markings hops up a water elm.

I never see Lewis Island without remembering a camping trip here with my friend Augustus, in his Carolina Skiff. We had put in at Morris Landing one Saturday morning with a full tank of gas, along with some extra gallons, with the goal of reaching the coast 112 miles away before sunset.

This was in the days before we became fully aware of what fossil fuels are doing to Earth's climate. We had signs—a three-year drought, for example—but we hadn't yet interpreted those signs, so we were still frivolous with gasoline. Those days are over, of course, and the days of the kayak and the canoe are upon us. But this story happened back in the Wasteful Age, when we believed that what we learned and what we taught others was more important than greenhouse gases in the atmosphere.

We flew down the coastal plain toward the ocean. We were going about fifteen miles an hour, skimming, blind to whatever might be in the water. Every riffle was possible danger—a snag, or a rock, or a sunken vessel. If the water had been lower, we would not have been able to speed like that, but we'd had plenty of rain and the floodplain was, well, flooded.

We reached Lewis Island before we had to stop for the night. A gaggle of wood storks and white ibis filled one of the cattail ponds bordering Lewis Creek. By the time we found a camping spot that did not look malarial, it was 8:00 p.m. and we had been on the water twelve hours, traveling full-bore most of that time. The campsite was a quarter acre carved out of wilderness, designated primitive camping. The spot was in a hardwood hammock, with maple, sweet gum, and saw palmetto next to a canebrake, posted "No camping behind this sign." Mosquitoes prospered.

No one would climb the bank onto Lewis Island without first rustling the bushes for snakes with a paddle. Lewis Island smelled like snakes. Normally I am not afraid of them, but this island had snake written all over it, the rich delta earth cut away to expose twisted, shaking, muscled roots. We tied up between two such-rooted trees.

Deep swamp is a dark art, a low-down blues, inner demons with tight holds. Everything is root and mud and twist. At low tide roots lie like the skeleton of a thing exposed, suddenly glinting, hard and soft at the same time. Cypress knees stand in beauty against soft mud, like small people waiting, with no need to speak to each other.

We made camp, boiled shrimp and ears of corn, then dropped the back anchor so that fast-passing motorboats wouldn't dash our vessel onto shore and strand us. By then the mosquitoes were epidemic.

Sometime in the night I woke to the sound of Augustus fumbling for the zipper of the tent we shared.

"What is it?" I asked. I heard a strange, loud, unsettling noise.

Augustus didn't answer, and I guessed that he was trying to be quiet.

"Augustus," I whispered. "What is that?"

He still didn't say anything.

"Are you listening to that?" I asked. What I heard was an eerie sound of multiple voices, talking among themselves. It sounded as if one lectured and others would answer or echo, muttering agreement. The sound was haunting.

"It's people," Augustus said, quietly and matter-of-factly and rather ominously.

"Isn't it owls?" I said.

"No, it's people."

"Can they be having church out here?" I asked. The clamor sounded like a church service, out in the wild wild wilderness.

Augustus said nothing, listening.

"That can't be church," I said. "We're too far in the woods." I wasn't asleep and neither was I imagining things. Far off a great horned owl hooted.

Was it a cult party?

Outside the tent, in the cool night, Augustus and I stood under a moonless sky obscured by the branches of trees, and we listened hard.

Then I understood.

"Frogs," I said, and slowly a grin spread across Augustus's face.

It was a hallelujah chorus of frogs, an almighty uproar. Every kind of frog call imaginable was sounding at once and they made a holy din.

Hallelujah, hallelujah. Speak the gospel, sister. Loud and clear. Tell it, brother, tell it. Don't hold back. Hallelujah.

"I had my pistol ready," he said.

"I've never heard anything like it."

"They must drive themselves mad."

The next day we got back in the motorboat, poured gasoline from one of the big plastic jugs in the back into the gas tank, and kept flying east. Once, we spotted something swimming ahead of us across the river.

"It's people," I said ominously.

"They're having church," Augustus said.

It was a wild hog, proof that hogs do swim. And believe me when I say frogs speak in tongues.

༂ I'm remembering this as we river paddlers reach Poppell's Bluff, called Old Bluff Joyner on the topo maps and renamed for Tom Poppell, a "good ole boy" sheriff of Darien who came into power in 1948 and was made infamous by Melissa Fay Greene's book *Praying for Sheetrock*. This bluff, apparently, was a popular party place for his cohorts, who were brought to mind by the frog cacophony. Pulling up, I spot immediately a huge potshard of ancient Guale origin, thick and crude. The Guale were an indigenous chiefdom along littoral Georgia and the Sea Islands; they were present when Spanish friars began settling the territory starting around 1568. They descended from prehistoric peoples who lived in the area for thousands of years. Disease and geopolitical pressures decimated the Guale, who eventually are thought to have merged into the Yemassee. Subsequent porings over the bluff lead us to more shards, smaller and mostly the thinner, more modern artifact.

Where Lewis Creek reenters the river, we fall out in the shallow current with a cold drink, thanks to Charlie. The water feels good, the drink refreshing. I have poison ivy on the backs of my hands, up my legs, and on the tops of my feet, which had to come from Hannah's Island, but not even poison ivy mars my joy.

As we chill in the river, Charlie says forget nature, that I should write Cracker romances, I could get rich.

"I'd be too ashamed," I say.

"Use a pseudonym."

"All the strippers have one," somebody else says.

"You know how to come up with a stripper name?" says Lola.

"No."

"You use the name of your first pet, followed by the street you lived on as a child."

"I'd be Lassie Jones," someone says.

"Dusty Bronson," says Raven.

"Blackie Hatch," I say.

"That sounds more like a serial killer," says Charlie. "By the way, have y'all noticed that serial killers always seem to have 'Wayne' as a middle name?"

"Oh Lord," Dave says. "My name is Dave Wayne."

We consider camping at the spot, but we opt instead to ease east to an island that some in our group remember from twenty years past. The island is named after a long-ago beloved named Vivian and is situated across from Butler Island. Vivian Island, however, is disappointing. It's spoil, a big pile of white sand littered with broken glass—not the worn and beautiful beach glass but the trashy glass glass.

"This is where we're spending the night?" I ask.

"If we go on, I don't know when we'd get to more high land," says Crawfish. "We don't need to be forced to sleep in the swamp."

"No, that wouldn't be good."

"Should we go back?"

"That seems difficult," says Lola.

"Back is upstream," says Raven.

"Plus it's getting late," I say.

"What does everybody think?" asks Dr. Presley, the egalitarian and the parliamentarian. As a matter of honor, none of us calls him by his first name. It's an unspoken decision. He is "Dr. Presley."

"We can manage here," someone says. We all agree.

We drag our boats through a mucky yucky belt of tidal silt, up a big hill. It is a nasty job and we get filthy, covered with quick-drying mud, the blackest of black. The bugs are terrible.

"I wouldn't wish this place on my worst enemy," I say.

For the first time all week, I'm dizzy. My body, so used to responding to the pitching of water, will not stop responding. The world is the river now, and I am rowing through it.

After we set up the tent, Raven and I sit and draw flowers—clematis on the riverbank, and marsh mallow toward the sand. Afterward we wander back into a scrub forest to gather bits of firewood, and there we hear a quick strange rushing sound. We find a barred owl feather, lying among brown leaves and deadwood under a newly green sweet gum. The sand is tracked by bobcat.

Found Objects:
pair of women's sandals, live-bait well for a boat, plastic yellow sand shovel, bungee cord, gar skull, softshell turtle skeleton, boys briefs, blue beer bottle, barred owl feather.

The Eighth Day

Saturday morning. Now we are close to the end. We solemnly eat our last breakfast together and break camp one final time. We drift quietly, separate, introspective, beneath Interstate 95. The roar of traffic, car after car, interspersed with eighteen-wheel trucks, is tremendous, and the bridge is a painful reminder of the uncivilization we are about to reenter. We are hanging on to a different life, a history, in the middle of an industrial age that will blindly erase the past.

This is my second time drifting into Darien. My friend Augustus and I had almost reached the town on our motorboat trip when the engine started faltering. Augustus scooted back to the motor and fiddled with it. The engine sputtered, and sputtered some more, then got going. We traveled a few hundred feet, then the motor sputtered again.

Within sight of the Highway 99 bridge, close to town, the engine stopped altogether. Augustus was tinkering with it, pulling on its cord, when a boat approached, a redheaded woman at the helm. It was Carolyn Hodges, with two guests in her boat.

Carolyn Hodges was the fiery innkeeper of Open Gates Bed and Breakfast. Her hair was dyed flame red, although it was more a rusty orange, like a wild seaweed steeped in iron. At any moment, her hair said, Carolyn might surprise you.

Born in the North, schooled at Middlebury College, Carolyn had come south and purchased an inn in the soporific coastal town. She settled the inn with old and beautiful things, antique furniture, and painstakingly embroidered linens. Then, surprisingly, she became a boat captain so she could run her guests up and down the river. She was a fierce advocate of the Altamaha, a founding member of Altamaha Riverkeeper.

"What in heaven's name are you two doing out here?" she asked.

"Drifting into Darien," Augustus chuckled.

Carolyn raised her thin and perfect eyebrows. "I see that. Engine trouble?" She had kept her figure over the years, and her clothing was tasteful.

"It just started sputtering."

"Sounds like the gas is bad," she said. "You want a tow in?" A tow, especially a tow from a woman, is the last thing most men want.

"We'll get her running again," Augustus said.

Carolyn had taken her guests to see the old cypress on Lewis Island, and they were wide-eyed, silent. Maybe they were from another country. All of this was probably not the pleasant little outing they imagined—the journey to the old cypress is not a cheery stroll but a slog through deep black mud and a torment of biting insects. Now here were two crazies stranded.

We thanked Carolyn and she pulled away.

We managed to get the motor started and we puttered into Darien. We staggered and stumbled into Darien.

If the Hardcore Heavyweights were to keep going, drifting, past the tabby buildings of the old town, out to the ocean, we would see more amazing things. I know this, too, because of the trip with Augustus. He and I bought new gas at the fish house and funneled it into the engine. After that, the boat ran like a charm. We left Darien and kept going. We made it all the way to Egg Island, at the firth of the Altamaha. I mean, we could have got out among the breakers and actually touched the shore of Egg Island, although we didn't. Behind us was Wolf Island. This place is one of forty unspoiled places internationally deemed "critical" for nesting shorebirds by the Western Hemisphere Shorebird Reserve Network. Egg and Wolf islands support 55,000 nesting shorebirds a year. The abundance of menhaden, a fish that lives in the surrounding waters, allows such numbers of birds to exist here.

I wept to think we had made it to the ocean, all the way down the Altamaha. The beach was filled with thousands of birds, kaleidoscopic, with a great, uproarious crying. Royal terns came in and out from sea, pogies in their beaks. A shrimp boat passed with pelicans riding its rails.

In our kayaks, we won't go all the way to the ocean. I've seen that fecund shore and would like to see it again, but not this time. Our vehicles are in Darien, our jobs are waiting. From Darien, the river goes on without us.

∿ Back among strangers, the memory of the crime returns. We have to go back and face all that happened. We will have to open our mail, even unusual packages, with a metallic taste in our mouths. We have to learn to love letters again, since most of them, 99.9 percent of them, are good. Raven will have to hook his fingers to a lie-detector machine and answer questions that people in uniform will ask. They will unhook the machine early and tell him they never believed he was the culprit. We will lock our doors. We will lie in bed, thinking of people we know, wondering.

A week or two later, a shiny black vehicle will wend down our woods driveway, and two men in black suits will disembark. They will flash badges that say Secret Service and will ask to see my husband, who is at work. They will tell me that a death threat signed by him has been sent to the president of the United States.

The president. This is the *Secret Service*. I will stay very calm and polite. I will invite the men inside. They will decline.

The letter says, "Dear Mr. Bush, your not a responsable person so I am going to kill you."

I will explain to the men in black that a copy was sent to the governor also, who is a Mr. Bush as well, which of course they know, and that my husband has already been investigated, that he has been exonerated. I will say that obviously the crime was directed against us, that the Florida investigators realized the entire time that my husband had not written the letter. I will tell them we have no idea who the culprit is. I will tell them where my husband can be found if they wish to speak with him.

A badness wants to know the light of day. It will not stay buried and silent. Whoever buried it will forever need to kick dirt back over it.

The person wronged will forever be trying to forgive.

A person will telephone us during the strange time following the writing of the hate letter. This is a person we do not know well. We both will hear this person say my husband's name in a mocking way. He will use the name signed in type on the letter, which is not the name my husband usually uses.

We will guess that this person, who is not our enemy, acted erringly on behalf of someone who perceived us as an enemy: that is the only motive we can untangle. The investigators will not find substantial evidence to charge anyone. No one confesses. And that will be the end of it.

But all that is in the future, straight ahead of us.

❧ Many people have known far greater threats. Many have known greater terror. The event of the letter, wretched though it was and disruptive to our lives, was minor in the grand view.

It helped me realize that there are two kinds of power. One is power *over*, held in place by victimization and oppression. The other power is *personal* power, the ability to make one's life go well, to make good decisions. Raven and I had no control over the posting of a venomous letter; we could, however, control our response and by doing so, reclaim our personal power. We could become more aware (not necessarily wary). We could take positive steps to protect ourselves. We could choose, as Wangari Maathai suggests, to exist somewhere beyond fear. "Evil" spelled backward is "live."

We could brood among the ruins or we could rebuild.

We chose to rebuild, keeping in mind that the world is awash in good deeds, in goodness, in gentleness and generosity and greatness. That's where the river was vital. By the time we drifted into Darien, we had rebuilt ourselves into better people. For eight days we witnessed moment by moment that nature is incapable of premeditated badness. Or goodness, for that matter. A river can't scheme.

Nor can a river forgive.

A river can't forgive because it is only capable, in the first place, of love. A river loves the dumpers, the polluters, the slayers, the nest-thieves, the bird-killers, the dammers, the water-stealers. A river loves even the clear-cutters.

But I can forgive.

I am trying to be like the river.

⁓ The last few hundred yards on the Altamaha River we don't paddle, we float, bows pointed eastward toward the ever-heating sun. We disembark near Darien's shrimp docks and pull our boats under a shade tree. We walk into town to find telephones, to call for rides, and we eat at a little cafe along the waterfront. Slowly our friends depart. My parents arrive to shuttle us back to the Baxley farm, and the next day we will pick up our truck from Murdock McRae's Landing, where our river odyssey began.

And that will be the end of it.

⁓ Except the river goes on.

O river. River of goodness. River of love.

Friend.

BOOK II *Elements*

"Perhaps in smaller ways than death, we lose the soul, a piece at a time, as when we turn away from what needs our help, remain silent when words are necessary, or take something from the world that can't be replaced—a plant, an animal, a love."
—Linda Hogan, *The Woman Who Watches Over the World*

Conversion

The flatheads have multiplied like Jesus's fish.
Enough to feed every soul except they are polluted
by something white and gluey
that the pulp mill drains into the water.
As they multiply they squeeze out the natives.
Like you and me,
scared to eat the channels, the shad,
the disappearing redbreasts
for fear of becoming destroyers.

Irwin Corbitt Tells Me How to Catch Catfish

Fish downstream.
Try to fish vertically.
Worms catch shellcrackers, bream, and small catfish.
Put a limb line at the *end* of a sandbar. Use shiners.
Catfish like crayfish.
They'll even bite soap.
The month of May is prime time for fishing soaplines.
Octagon is best. Put it in the microwave to soften it.
Most people just use Ivory.

CHAPTER 1 *Endangered Landscape*

I.

Malcolm Hodges wants to buy the whole river, all 137 miles of it.

"We're talking about a million acres," he says. He is eating a big, oval, glazed bun as we drive riverward, although his mind is not on the treat.

"Where?" I ask. "You could buy a million acres of headwaters."

"I mean the whole river, the length of it," he says. "Land contiguous. But not simply a corridor."

"Wider than a corridor?"

"A landscape," he says.

"What would you do with it?" I ask.

"We'd protect it," he says, between bites of the sweet, which he's just purchased at the Mennonite bakery in Jesup, where we met. "We'd restore it."

"A million acres would offer the protection the river needs?" I ask.

"It would be a good start."

It is the middle 1990s and the "we" to whom Malcolm refers is The Nature Conservancy (TNC), a conservation nonprofit that works to preserve natural areas and in whose employ I have discovered many good friends. Malcolm works as a biologist for the Georgia chapter. TNC has a name for this visionary new idea, that of protecting an entire landscape. In 1991 it named the basin a "bioreserve."

A million acres is how big the Altamaha Bioreserve should be, Malcolm is saying. We're talking the size of Glacier National Park. Bigger than Rhode Island.

"So much land protection is haphazard," he says. "Somebody notices a nice area and it gets saved. We're taking a geographically defined area—the basin of a river—and we're looking at it systematically to find *everything* worth saving."

Wow. The Nature Conservancy is not trying to safeguard the water itself or its immediate floodplain, or even isolated tracts along it. It wants the entire landscape protected. That's a dream I can believe in.

At the time that I find myself riding riverward with Malcolm, I have returned recently to south Georgia and am engaged in a course in miracles of my own design. I am determined to learn all I can about my homeland. This day with Malcolm is class. I'm the student.

Malcolm looks similar to what I imagined from hearing his voice on the phone, when I called to ask if he had time to tell me about his work. He's in his midthirties, medium-built, with brown curly hair. He is wearing a T-shirt promoting the Mississippi Native Plant Society, and is indeed a Mississippian. His father, who worked in the shipyard at Pascagoula, was a fine outdoorsman. "If biophilia is genetic I get it from my father," Malcolm said. He studied ornithology at Mississippi State.

The month is August, and August means misery in the South, so we have started early.

"About this bioreserve," I say. "How will you identify important land?" My sensible bran muffin deserves more attention than I'm paying it.

"We've done an assessment," Malcolm says. "At the end of 1993, TNC completed a biological inventory that included mapping plant communities along both sides of the river and determining the status of rare plants and animals."

Prior to this study, Malcolm says, it was well known that a rich menagerie of animal life found refuge in diverse plant communities along the Altamaha's creeks, oxbows, and sloughs. Forty rare species had been documented along the river in 87 precise locations. In the inventory, funded by the Woodruff Foundation, ninety-eight species of rare plants and animals in 465 locations were identified.

This proved that the Altamaha supports, as TNC called it, the *largest documented aggregation of globally imperiled elements of any watershed in Georgia*. Of the ninety-eight rare species, thirteen are federally listed and another fourteen protected by the state.

These findings encouraged The Nature Conservancy to designate the Altamaha River corridor as one of the world's "75 Last Great Places."

Not Georgia's. Not America's. *The world's*.

Seventy-five great places are left, and my river is one of them.

"So give me an example," I say.

"Of imperiled species?"

"Yes."

"Radford's *dicerandra* is a small mint that grows in two locations in the world, both in McIntosh County along Altamaha sand ridges," says Malcolm. "It's federally protected but grows on private land. Hopefully we'll see some."

"That would be great."

"Another is *Franklinia altamaha*, a rare flowering shrub discovered in 1765 by William Bartram and not seen in the wild since."

"I've heard of *Franklinia*," I say.

"You know, then, that we won't see it today."

"Unfortunately," I say.

"We'd have to drive a long way to see that one," Malcolm says.

"So you've done the biological assessment. You know what's here. What happens next?" I ask.

"We recently finished a conservation plan," Malcolm says. "That outlines our mission and our strategy. Now we're working on actual protection—through purchase, conservation easements, and private landowner agreements. Some places, of course, are already protected."

"By TNC?"

"By the state, before we came on the scene."

"Such as?"

"Let's see. Big Hammock Wildlife Management Area, Bullard Creek. Then there's Wolf Island; it's a National Wildlife Refuge. The Altamaha River Waterfowl Area."

Big Hammock, for example, is over 1,300 acres of land bordering the river that Rayonier, the timber company, donated to the state in

1978. The Altamaha River Waterfowl Area, a freshwater tidal swamp, contains 22,000 acres near Darien. Several river islands are part of the tract, including Lewis, where the 1,000-year-old cypress still stand.

"So you're not starting at ground zero."

"No. Thousands of acres are already protected. We're well on the way toward a million."

"That you want to work with an entire watershed is so exciting," I say.

I haven't been watching the roads, attending to note taking instead, and I look up to see we're in old Georgia. Large weather-beaten farmhouses are set amidst green pastures. We come to a red brick church with a hillside graveyard, then a sign that says "Old River Road."

"Most of this river basin used to be pine woodlands, rolling terrain, maintained by natural fire," Malcolm is saying. "It's mostly converted to pine plantations."

He isn't telling me anything I don't know. I know all about the destruction of the longleaf pine, an ecosystem that is 99 percent demolished.

"You find an area with a bit of natural woods and you're happy," he says. When he says "you," I know he means "I." "There's one there." He points to an acre or two of woods. "Just little patches here and there. And that's all that's left."

"I do the same thing," I say. "When I travel, I look for natural forest. All the time. Real woods are rare, and seeing some is cause to celebrate. Then you come along two weeks later and they're gone."

"All you have to do is invoke the J word and they get cut," Malcolm continues.

I look at him, quizzical. "J?"

"Jobs."

"Oh. I thought you meant Jesus."

"No," says Malcolm.

"Jesus would not destroy creation," I say.

At our first stop, a bluff, Malcolm pulls out an infrared map of the river corridor taken in winter. The map is predominantly a dull liver-red. The red reflects pine plantations, Malcolm says, like those through which we've been traveling.

"This is what I was talking about," he says. The basin is riddled with wounds.

"Where we are now, this bluff," Malcolm says, "is intact. These are southern mixed hardwoods. We're here on the map, in this thumb-print of green." The river, its entire length, he says, is flanked occasionally by bluffs, some as high as one hundred feet, that shape-shift as the river twists. We are parked atop one of them.

"A bluff forest is naturally eroding," Malcolm says.

"Meaning?"

"Trees fall in the water. It's the nature of the ecosystem. The bluff shifts."

I'm writing it all down.

"These bluffs are very diverse, especially the north side," he says, and begins to name flora common to them: Darlington oak, southern magnolia, hop hornbeam, sweet gum, water hickory, water oak, white oak, sparkleberry, witch hazel, American olive, beech, flame azalea, arrowwood (straight-shafted—Indians used to make arrows from it), maple, loblolly, and spruce pine.

"Okay, let's have a look around."

Not ten feet from the truck, Malcolm lets out a yelp. It's our first rare plant, *Matelea alabamensis*, or Alabama milkvine, a milkweed known to exist in about five locations in Georgia. It no longer exists in Alabama, chiefly due to the clearing of hardwood forests. This specimen doesn't look prosperous; its light-green leaves appear sickly.

"It's hanging on," Malcolm says.

We hike along the bluff and then down to the water, stopping to pick and eat muscadines, flushing a yellow-billed cuckoo and a pileated woodpecker, and coming to squat beneath a willow to stare at the river. The water's high and wide, four to five hundred feet across, and fast. The summer has been wet.

"This time of year the river should be moseying along," says Malcolm.

Flooding, however, is what has preserved much of the Altamaha floodplain. During rainy months (especially winter, but sometimes eight months a year, and climate change is messing up those cycles too) the floodplain is inundated and river access is limited. Further toward the ocean the river widens to as much as five miles in the rainy season, and even here inland, the floodplain stretches almost a mile.

Today is Malcolm's lucky day. He finds two quarters, both heads up.

"You have one," he says, and hands me a coin.

"Thanks."

"Look up," Malcolm says. A swallow-tailed kite pirouettes above the river, a rare sight of an exceptional species. We walk in beauty.

We get back in the truck to continue our tour. Farther along we stop to watch a gopher tortoise, a federally threatened species since 1987 in areas west of Mobile, Alabama, and under review for listing in other parts of the South. The land tortoise requires mature, open forests through which it can travel easily, feeding on grasses and other vegetation. Absence of fire and clear-cutting of forests, both of which result in thickly tangled undergrowth, have been primary factors in the tortoise's decline.

"Aerial photos of the entire region were taken in 1988," Malcolm says, "so we know which places have been clear-cut since 1988. They're *mining* the timber around here."

We come out on a dirt road and see a ridge.

"Generally, changes in the coastal plain are not very dramatic," Malcolm says. "This is cool."

∾   Malcolm gives up most of his day. I don't think he begrudges it, because he lives in Darien, population under two thousand, where not much happens. For movies he goes to Brunswick.

At one place he pulls off Highway 144 to show me the globally imperiled Georgia plume, *Ellioti racemosa*, a heath first observed by Bartram in 1773, known to occur in about three dozen locations in Georgia. Here it is growing on the shoulder of the road, in a sand ridge. It blooms plumal white flowers and turns its leaves upright in bright light. This morning its leaves are horizontal. The ground below is sprinkled with earth star, a fungus that lies in constellations on the ground in sandhills. Cousin to the puffball, it is a double-layered sphere filled with spores, and its outer layer splits open like a star. In all the years I was away from Georgia, I missed the earth star.

Early afternoon we cross Beards Creek and pull into Adamson's Fish Camp and Beards Bluff Campground, which is announced by a fading sign. We picnic on Mama's salmon salad, wheat bread from the bakery, potato chips, and cookies amid an inland maritime forest of live oaks, magnolia, and palmetto.

Spanish moss hangs from the live oak branches. "The trees hereabout have all their branches draped with it," John Muir wrote of the bromeliad in *A Thousand-Mile Walk to the Gulf*, the account of a trek he undertook in 1867, "producing a remarkable effect."

Malcolm and I ease down to the water. The landing is starting to buzz with boats coming in. I take off my shoes—we've done a lot of walking—and dip my feet in the swollen river.

"Seven endemic mussels are found nowhere else on the planet but in the Altamaha River Basin," Malcolm says. "One, the Altamaha spiny mussel, is under consideration for federal listing."

I'm taking notes. "Names of others?"

He rolls words off his tongue: Altamaha lance, Altamaha slabshell, Georgia elephant ear, Altamaha pocketbook, Altamaha arc mussel, rayed pink fatmucket, Savanna lilliput.

"Rayed pink fatmucket?" I asked, "Who named that one?"

"Some old heavy-drinking mussel scientist a while back," Malcolm answers. He laughs, then pauses. "Let's get this tick out of your hair."

He tells about seining Beards Creek, a tributary of the river, and finding twenty-five to thirty species of fish. "Kind of incredible for such a little creek," he says. "Oh, and the only viable population of shortnose sturgeon in the world is in the Altamaha. They spawn around Jesup."

"Viable?"

"With a healthy reproduction rate. And the river's a regulated fishery for Atlantic sturgeon." Another motorboat coughs to a whining start.

Malcolm is a veritable inventory of the river's biota, a walking encyclopedia of natural history. As we sit on its banks, he speaks of heartbreak and of promise for the place. His language and tone, however, are dispassionate, disengaged, scientific. With my toes in the water, digesting lunch, I ask him what the river means to him. Does all the cutting and polluting weigh on his heart?

"It's a project to me," he says. "I get buried in the data."

He is silent a minute, and I let the silence settle. I am reclaiming the Altamaha, its wind and water on me, its sand beneath my bare feet.

"I think my detachment might be a little deliberate," Malcolm finally says. "All I'm doing is watching beautiful, irreplaceable, mature pine woodlands and swamp forests get axed. Rafting down the Altamaha is a religious experience, especially in the spring. There are fresh green leaves on the cypress trees. The swamps are as beautiful a place as you can think of. It gives you goose bumps to see them."

He rises to his feet, ready to drive on. "It's tough working here," he says. "You have to take the bitter with the sweet."

II.

That day on the river with Malcolm Hodges took place in the early days of the Altamaha Bioreserve. Soon after, I met Christi Lambert, who directs the project. Christi is dynamite, a powerhouse in a tiny frame. She is steady as a rock and she works ceaselessly toward her goals. I have never seen her waver. I have never seen her angry, either, always soft-spoken and positive. Christi can be counted on for rational, sensible thinking.

As the years passed, under Christi's leadership and the sound ecological guidance of Alison McGee, the success of TNC's project mounted. The organization purchased acre after acre, most of which passed into the hands of the state or federal government and thus under its protection. It secured conservation easements on other acres. Steadily, relentlessly, single-mindedly, Christi and TNC staff maneuvered their pawns and horses one move at a time, until a deal was in checkmate. They raised funds from state, federal, and private sources. They closed.

Instead of a king being crowned, a kingdom grew.

I have become wonderful friends with Christi. Our collaborations have been a rich part of my life. Not long ago I was talking to her. She had been out on the water with a funder, surveying the success. "It's thrilling," she said, "to see how we've been able to knit together these pieces."

As of 2011, twenty years after the project began, almost 100,000 acres in the Altamaha Bioreserve have been protected. In late 2010 TNC purchased 14,000 more acres, including Bug Island, from Rayonier. Of the $24 million purchase price, $4.7 million was contributed by the Robert W. Woodruff Foundation, which has bequeathed more than $12 million toward the Altamaha Bioreserve over the years.

When the deal was signed, statewide director Shelly Lakly announced that only one small parcel of land separated TNC from a huge milestone, the connection of forty-one contiguous river miles and 100,000 acres along the Altamaha River. "The Altamaha River, being so remote, is essential to our coast remaining healthy," Lakly said. "There's no development. It's a beautiful, living, breathing place. Some of the cypress trees along the river are believed to be twelve hundred years old."

We're nowhere near the million-acre mark. We're only one-tenth of the way there. But a miracle has happened.

The Nature Conservancy saw the Altamaha as a place worth saving.

They decided to save it.

Nothing will ever be the same.

CHAPTER 2 *River Sticks*

I seek the darkest wood, the thickest and most interminable and, to the
citizen, most dismal swamp. I enter a swamp as a sacred place,—a *sanctum
sanctorum*. There is the strength, the marrow, of Nature.
—Henry David Thoreau, from "Walking"

Folks, we have us a problem. Scientists have spent a long time studying and deduced a fact that any of my neighbors could have told them already—*a river is only as healthy as the forests along it*. That means the Altamaha is in trouble. Because we're cutting its forests to death.

You know by now how attached I am to this watershed. It created me. Its water flows in my bones, which are composed of minerals the river bore down from the Appalachians. My history is here, as is my present, and likely my future, so when Malcolm Hodges showed me the map that had our forest-blood all over it, like a big blood pudding with a river running down the center, I had to find out more.

I tried to find some forest figures that are clear-cut, so to speak. I went first to the US Forest Service, the people some of you might assume would be in charge of keeping our forests in good working order but who are actually the management office for cutting them down, and I asked about statistics. It turns out that the Southern Research Station in Asheville, a unit of the Forest Service, has been counting and measuring trees in Georgia for a few years.

The scientists there told me that as of 2004, Georgia had the most forest cover of any state in the South, with 67 percent. Sixty-seven percent of the state is forest.

"Something's not right," I told one of them. "I live in Georgia, and not in any city, and I bet you my grandpa's twenty-dollar gold piece that 67 percent of Georgia is not forest."

"Oh, yes, ma'am, it is," the scientist said.

"I'm telling you," I said, "this state is not two-thirds forest, no matter how you crank the numbers."

"According to our definition, it is."

"What is your definition?" I asked. And I was referred to a Web site, srsfia2.fs.fed.us—Southern Research Station's Forest Inventory and Analysis for Georgia.

"Forestland," according to the US Forest Service Georgia fact sheet, is "land at least ten percent stocked by forest trees of any size, or formerly having had such tree cover." Whoa, stop there. What is 10 percent stocked? Does that mean that if you own ten acres, and one of those acres has trees on it, the entire ten acres is a forest?

And excuse me, when they say "stocked," I think of a fish pond. We're talking about sacred places where, Saint Bernard promised, wisdom is found. "You will find something more in woods than in books," he said, and he didn't mean an empty logging truck.

Let's go back to the tract I asked about. If that one acre in question *formerly* had trees on it, the entire piece is still a ten-acre forest?

All this time I've been thinking a forest was something else. I thought a forest was a thick growth of trees covering an extensive tract of land. I thought a forest held trees of all kinds and ages, sapling to old growth, and among those trees grew beaucoup underbrush— shrubs and wildflowers—and among all that flora lived drifts of birds and crashes of animals and ambushes of insects and schools of fish. I was thinking like Rabindranath Tagore, "Trees are the earth's endless effort to speak to the listening heaven." And again like Saint Bernard, "Trees and stones will teach you that which you can never learn from masters." I was thinking about never seeing a poem lovely as a tree.

And I'm telling you, 67 percent of my state is not the earth trying to speak to the listening heaven.

Most of it is made up of places for the devil to hide.

The government (meaning the Forest Service) had more definition. It said that a piece of land, furthermore, must be at least an acre in size to be called a forest, and "forest strips" must be at least 120 feet wide. OK, that's good. That means my front yard can't be classified as forest, but the minimum requirements are a bit low, don't you think? What on earth is a forest strip? Like a chicken strip? "The forest strip primeval" and "forest strips ancient as the hills?"

"So the kind of trees on the land doesn't matter?" That was me.

"No, a tree is a tree."

I'm no scientist, but I know that there's a tree and then there's a tree. I can take you to a place deep in the swamp and show you a tree. Let me know when you want to go. I don't mean to be rude, but I don't understand why we call you guys the Forest *Service*. This sounds like the Forest *Dis*service.

At least I've found the problem: the people who are counting what forest we have left are fudging. They're warping the rules. They're making something sound better than it is.

I found a table called "Average Annual Timberland Disturbances."

"Disturbance," it seems, is the word used for death. Some of the disturbances are human-caused, and these are termed "treatments." Treatments include "final harvest," which sounds a hell of a lot like clear-cutting to me. The government-salaried timber barons don't even have the guts to call clear-cutting by its real name. They call it "final harvest" or they call it "even-aged timber management," a screwball takeoff on "uneven-aged timber management." That one really makes me angry. Uneven-aged timber management is the only kind of ecological timber harvesting I know. It means going into a forest and selecting individual trees for cutting—trees that are diseased, leaning, too close to others, free of endangered animals, mature. It's hard work, which most people want to avoid. And it's intelligent.

Other government "treatments" are "partial harvest," which translates to coming back as soon as the ground's dry enough, and "thinning," which means the deer and turkeys have a few years yet.

Just so you know, the average annual final harvest is 430,000 acres. Let me interpret. Four hundred thirty thousand acres in Georgia annually are "disturbed" by a "treatment" that calls for "even-aged management" and ends in 430,000 acres of fricking clear-cut. "Amazing Grace" and follow the casket down the aisle. Yea, though I canoe through the valley of the shadow of death, thou art with me. May the circle be unbroken.

Another 161,000 acres on average are sacrificed to partial harvest, and 199,000 are thinned.

Something else about the mazes and tables concocted by the Forest Service confounds me. Of the 24.8 million acres in the state that are in forest cover (even if that means only 10 percent *stocked*, or *former* forest cover, or both) only 6.5 million acres are in planted pine. That's 27 percent of all timberland. That makes no sense because I know what I know, I see what I see.

Come on, people. You're saying only one-fourth of the state's "forests" are planted pine? A statement like that makes me almost blind with anger. What I want to know is, where are those 18.3 million acres of real forest? I've been looking for them a long time and I want to see some of them.

Here's an agency that hides its wrongdoing and protections of wrongdoers behind nuance, rhetoric, doublespeak, and skewed statistics.

I could go on and on about the deceptions of the US Forest Service when it comes to convincing us uneducated southerners what's not going on in our woods. But if you take enough time, and you read the tables closely enough, you'll see the holes. You'll see that the majority of pines in 2004 were nine inches or smaller in diameter, and that pines larger than twenty inches in diameter are scarce as snowmen. Large cypress are almost nonexistent.

In 2004 University of California professor George Lakoff wrote a book called *Don't Think of an Elephant!: Know Your Values and Frame the Debate*. Lakoff is a cognitive linguist. He studies the ways we use language in this country to manipulate, flummox, and hoodwink the American citizenry, and he tries to train his readers to look for the lingo. One hand is waving a magic wand while the other slips a hundred-dollar bill out of your pocket.

We can see when people are using Orwellian language. "But we should recognize," Lakoff writes, "that they use Orwellian language precisely when they have to: when they are weak, when they cannot just come out and say what they mean." My job as a writer, then, is to present the facts.

"People think in frames," Lakoff writes. "To be accepted, the truth must fit people's frames. If the facts do not fit a frame, the frame stays and the facts bounce off."

So let's frame this dialogue:

I'm going to be *honest* with you. We Americans *love* our forests. Forests are key to our *prosperity*. They ensure that we live in a *clean* and *healthy* and *safe* world. They are our *investment* in the future. They ensure *opportunity*. Cutting forests wholesale is not *fair* to us in any way—it's unfair to our *children*, unfair to our *neighbors*, unfair to our *communities*, unfair to ourselves. Forests have always been our *security*. Destroying the forests is *robbing* our children. We are being *robbed*. Taking away our forests is depriving *hardworking* Americans of *prosperity, opportunity, health*, and *security*.

᨞   A better figure for what's left is probably the calculation of the Georgia Department of Natural Resources (DNR).

I'm not a big fan of human-made objects cruising around the heavens, posturing as stars, falling every once in a while, but there's one thing for sure—logging can hide behind "private property" signs and beauty strips, but it can't hide from satellites. Using satellite images, biologists and statisticians in the Nongame Conservation Section of the Georgia DNR mapped out the state. We now have an accurate look at what's happening all around us, too close for us to see.

The DNR determined that 36 percent of the state is covered by vegetation in its natural condition. One-third of the state. Thirty-three percent of the coastal plain, where the Altamaha flows, is native vegetation. They didn't count beaches, dunes, suburbs, golf courses, hay pastures, row crops, mowed utility swaths, city streets, quarries, or strip mines, and no, they did not count pine plantations. "We believe that excluding them results in a more accurate depiction of lands in a natural state," DNR biologists wrote in their report. Thank you, DNR.

The map they made uses dark green for heavy natural vegetation. There's a big wedge in the mountains, which is the Chattahoochee National Forest. There's the Okefenokee Swamp. The coast, laden with fertile salt marshes and maritime hammocks, which are native vegetation, is dark. And through the center of the state is a thin valley that looks a bit like a Y, or a slingshot, and that is the corridor of the Altamaha, the part that gets flooded.

Everything else—everything—is lighter, the light green of altered landscapes. The river comes dark through its forested floodplain out of the heart of Georgia, through land that dims and pales with loss. We are cutting Georgia out of existence.

The rural South has been hard-hit environmentally. It has been colonized, another wave in a storm of colonizations that began with European conquest and indigenous dispossession. We mine the South for resources, becoming ever more tactical in our development of the tools of destruction.

꩜ In the half century before the 1950s, the kind of intensive clear-cutting we suffer today was abnormal. Landowners cut but rarely did they obliterate. They did not spray herbicide and bed rows so they could plant pines like we plant cotton. When I was growing up, in the 1960s and 1970s, people seemed to have affection and affinity for the woods and prided themselves on keeping their forests. Lord, where are those people now? They rest in their dry and dreary graves.

Now it's money we love. Damn the forests.

When the softwoods began to run out, the timber industry turned to hardwoods. As if losing our uplands wasn't criminal enough, our wetlands came under the same concerted, clear-cut-and-let-God-sort-it-out kind of attack. In the dry spells, which have been increasing in frequency and length, due to global warming, loggers began anew to go into wetlands—protected by law and sacred in the eyes of God—and cut. Cypress are ground up for yard mulch.

Imagine.

Does it not make you want to retch?

Humans have not always stood knee-deep in wetlands and appreciated them. Land that is periodically inundated has been considered by many worthless, good for nothing but holding the world together, and worse—breeding ground for disease, obstacle to progress. Crops can't be grown in standing water, nor cattle grazed, nor houses constructed.

Wetlands across the mainland United States declined from 221 million acres historically to 103 million in the mid-1980s. Since European settlement, half of the forested wetlands of the South (35 million acres) have been lost. Call them swamps or call them sloughs, they're gone.

"A 50 percent loss in wetlands," said Paul Moler, a Florida research biologist, "essentially represents a 50 percent loss in those species that live in wetlands." For example, the one-toed amphiuma, a strange and secretive foot-long salamander that haunts streambed muck, has suffered a 60 percent decline in populations since European settlement.

How are wetlands ruined? They are converted to drylands. Excessive amounts of water are withdrawn. They're logged. If we overlay drought atop these, we see a poignant scenario for wetland-dependent wildlife.

God knows what wetlands are good for. Water filtration. Flood control. Wildlife habitat. Concatenation in the chain of life. Beauty.

Every animal is dependent, to some degree, on wetlands. Some, like fish, live there. Others use them for drink. Some, like the gopher frog, live in the uplands but return to wetlands to breed. Bear move to wetlands in fall to fatten on the mast of tupelo and Ogeechee lime. Swallow-tailed kites nest in them. Dragonflies zip along. A mother gator guards a small pool, where her young, less than a foot long, float. Prothonotary warblers flit about calling "zweet, zweet, zweet." Folks, you're in a wetland.

Beaver dam. Yellow-crowned night heron rookery. Softshell turtle. Slider.

The success of sport fish is rooted in shallow-water fish, and the decline of wetlands has wrecked many fisheries.

Wetland loss is particularly hard on wading birds. The wood stork, for example, is a federally endangered bird highly adapted to specialized wetlands. Not just any old pond will do. The birds, which travel up to forty miles from their nest to feed, need what's called ephemeral wetlands, a sequence of pools that dry at different times. This is because they feed methodically. The bird wades through shallow water continuously opening and closing its bill, like Pac-Man. Whatever it happens to touch, it eats—mostly fish, but also the crawfish, amphibians, and snakes that happen to land in its scissorlike bill.

Numbers of little blue herons are down. Great blue herons are declining in parts of their range. Could it be that the wading birds are disappearing because the forests are being cut out from under them?

∿ Since we're talking about forests, I need to tell you about the latest assault.

In the mid-2000s I began to hear a term bandied about: biomass. It was an answer to climate change, which scientists increasingly feared would become runaway, and a panacea to the scarcity of energy sources for the future. The timber industry, hurting from the recession and a depressed market, needed a new boom. Desperate for solutions, people—even some well-meaning and well-educated ones—leapt on the biomass bandwagon.

Mostly what the industry was looking for were handouts from the government in the form of renewable energy credits.

That unencumbered government money—welfare checks for corporations—caused people to go a little mad.

First, let me explain biomass. Biomass is organic material from living or recently living organisms, which through photosynthesis stored energy from the sun. In common usage today, it is the cutting and burning of our forests and pine plantations to produce electricity.

Biomass is incineration. It's a big—a really big—burn barrel. Knowing nobody would want to live near an *incinerator*, the timber industry hid behind more obfuscation, this time "gasification" and "pyrolysis," which are fancy names for burning things.

The original sin is that government leaders at the Kyoto Conference, which sought to regulate greenhouse gas emissions globally, failed to embrace the fact that biomass is not "carbon neutral." Global warming, or more aptly, climate disruption, is caused by the buildup of carbon dioxide (CO_2) and other heat-trapping gases in the atmosphere, causing warming of the globe. Here was a source of power that people came to believe did not contribute to climate change, an answer to prayers. I have sat in audiences where speakers touted biomass as carbon neutral.

Excuse me?

The Kyoto Protocol established reduction targets for fossil fuels, but not for other types of energy. Not for biomass. Despite what the Kyoto conference overlooked, and what industry declares, biomass will never be carbon neutral, no matter how anyone spins it. To the extent that carbon can be regained by replanting forests, the recapture will take decades. Burning wood or any other organic fuel will *increase* global warming. Add to this the ancillary emissions that come from production, harvest, use, and transportation of biomass.

Ann Ingerson of Vermont, economist with The Wilderness Society, has been studying the role of forests in climate change. She reports that, far from being carbon neutral, biomass often releases more carbon than fossil fuels in the short run, for a net loss of atmospheric health. Only a few types of wood fuel can really come close to carbon neutrality—waste that would have decomposed quickly anyway if not used for energy; perennial energy crops planted on abandoned farmland; or thinnings that reduce fire frequency or severity. The rest depends on the removal of live trees, which transfers carbon from the biosphere to the atmosphere.

The slump of years represented by the time it takes a forest to regenerate, during which time most standing forests will have continued to absorb carbon, will yank us ever more quickly toward a disastrous climate crisis.

If a pine plantation containing twenty-five-year-old trees is cut and burned, then we must wait twenty-five years and a day for it to be carbon-neutralized. [Note: Because biomass releases more carbon than the natural gas or other fuel that would have been used instead, you do need to make up a bit extra beyond what you've removed from the forest; plus you could lose some soil carbon through harvest disturbances, and that needs to be replenished as well.] We cannot in this moment afford to put any more carbon dioxide into the atmosphere.

In addition, Ingerson told me, the Southeast is gearing up for massive exports of wood chips and pellets to Europe, in response to demand for carbon-neutral energy in those countries. Because climate regulations there define biomass burning as carbon neutral, and because nobody is responsible for reporting the emissions from ocean shipping, we have a rather bizarre situation in that we are using lots of energy and depleting forest carbon in *this* country in order to meet illusory climate targets in another.

At the Georgia River Network conference in 2010 I heard someone from the Southern Alliance for Clean Energy say, "Bioenergy is an important resource—particularly for baseload supply—for Georgia for reducing many toxic air pollutants as well as greenhouse gas emissions." The speaker actually boasted that burning down our forests will reduce greenhouse gases *as well as* air pollution. You name me a wood fire that doesn't give off CO_2 and I'll eat a church pew. All wood and other organic materials contain carbon, and burning them will confound the problems caused by greenhouse gases.

The burning of biomass is a major source of harmful pollutants including particulate matter, nitrogen oxides, carbon monoxide, heavy metals, sulfur dioxide, and numerous carcinogens.

Here is a partial list of pollutants that one biomass plant, proposed for operation in Georgia, applied for permission to release: hydrogen chloride, mercury, arsenic, lead, formaldehyde, ammonia, carbon monoxide, acrolein, benzene, beryllium, cadmium, chromium, manganese, nickel, and selenium, nitrogen oxide, particulate matter, volatile organic compounds, styrene, and metal air pollutants (not identified). Hundreds of distinct hazardous by-products are associated with biomass.

To support biomass as a clean energy is an affront to the word. To call biomass "alternative" is oxymoronic. To say this to my face is worse than slapping me. I'd rather you blacked my eye.

Yes, wood *in some ways* is better than coal. Harvesting it doesn't destroy the Appalachians, thought to be the oldest mountains in the world. Wood doesn't leave the coalfields of West Virginia, Kentucky, Tennessee, and Alabama in wretched poverty, in ill health—dying, in fact—in utter hopelessness because not only are their communities being destroyed, so are their landscapes. Wood doesn't release as much sulfur dioxide as coal.

Remember, however, that incinerators release more carbon dioxide in stack emissions per megawatt of energy than coal plants. Incinerators typically emit more greenhouse gas per kilowatt hour than gas-fired plants.

We need to get beyond incineration and combustion of all kinds. Incineration is what we're doing to the planet, and we need less of it.

Biomass is a weak-minded, money-driven, part-way solution to the most pressing problem we humans have ever had to face, which is the destruction of our very biosphere. By touting biomass, we artificially restrain viable alternatives and thus we limit our possibilities for lasting, long-term solutions. As Johann Hari wrote in his brilliant article, "The Wrong Kind of Green," in the March 22, 2010, issue of *The Nation*, "You can't jump halfway across a chasm: you still fall to your death. It is all or disaster."

Biomass currently is more corporate welfare in the form of government subsidies destroying the last remnants of our native forests before our very eyes, with no effects on mounting global temperatures and heightening weather catastrophes. Katherine Ling, of *Environment and Energy News*, reported on Aug. 24, 2009, that "The South could largely offset its growth in energy demands . . . through 2020 if it fully utilized 'cost-effective' energy efficiency measures."

Efficiency meaning using less. Turning things off. Unplugging shit.

"Efficiency technically could reduce demand by 2 percent per year," Ling said.

In his essay "Walking," Thoreau wrote, "A township where one primitive forest waves above while another primitive forest rots below—such a town is fitted to raise not only corn and potatoes, but poets and philosophers for the coming ages."

In my lifetime I have labored ceaselessly on behalf of the forests of the South, hoping to slow their demise and begin to see them restored. They have endured onslaught after onslaught—from turpentining to timbering the old growth, from chipping for pulp to tree farming. By 1995 the longleaf pine forests, for example, which historically occupied 93 million acres of the southern coastal plain, were 99 percent gone. Less than 1,000 acres of virgin longleaf pine remained in the region.

Few other ecosystems in this nation have suffered so egregious a slaughter.

Of 190 plants associated with longleaf uplands, 122 are threatened or endangered. The animals associated with longleaf pine—gopher tortoise, red-cockaded woodpecker, flatwoods salamander, Northern bobwhite quail, Bachman's sparrow, indigo snake—continue a staggering decline. They and others have the misfortune to join our pine flatwoods in their demise, which is a disappearance from the face of the earth. Even in my short lifetime I have borne witness to this. With the loss of our forests, our rural economies suffer (we are exporting our jobs), our communities suffer, our cultures suffer, our landscapes suffer, our health suffers.

We are suffering out here in rural Georgia—do you understand this?—watching our landscapes get shredded, chipped, pulped, reduced to muddy and torn-up ground.

～ The new cure-all is eucalyptus. I'm hearing proposals for replacing native forests with fast-growing, genetically modified, exotic monocultures. The perverse rationale is that select species grow faster and could be cultivated to generate more combustible fuel at a lower price per acre per year. Obviously, advocates of this approach view forests as nothing more than a cash cow. They have utterly no consideration of the ecological value of legitimate, functional highlands and lowlands. Likewise, the shorter "production cycle" would mean more-frequent clear-cutting, with associated erosion and water contamination.

At one of his town meetings (in Baxley, Georgia) I heard Republican US Representative Jack Kingston say that he wanted "Georgia to be the Saudi Arabia of pine."

Think about that a minute.

Jack Kingston is pretty much getting what he wants. We're getting desertification already, and another degree or two rise in global temperatures will get us a dessicated plain that used to be the lush, green, temperate-and-subtropical South.

What Georgia is not getting is the wealth.

If I know nothing else, I know this: *A pine plantation is not a forest, no matter what any forestry association tells you.* And, *a river is only as healthy as the ecosystems it drains.*

I will not be forced into silence while the forests I love get mowed to the ground by a society violently wasteful with its energy and unapologetic in its contagious greed. In my presence, I will not allow misinformation to be spread about practices that will continue to destroy these forests. I will not support halfway measures that will only serve to distract us from the steps vitally necessary to halt a runaway climate catastrophe and protect life on Earth.

⤳ But this story is about a river. Let's go back to the cool shade of the cypress and tupelo swamp. I'm doing my own research. Right now, as I write this, during late July, the temperature is 100 degrees on our porch. In the solar dehydrator it is 128. But down at the river, under the black willows, the temperature is ten degrees cooler. Ninety degrees.

Cut the trees and we mess up the world.

Leave the trees, keep the river. Keep the atmosphere. It's as simple as that.

CHAPTER 3 *Stewards of the Mysteries of God*

I have a story about a crab that started a movement. It is about a river that is stunning in its magnitude and in its biodiversity. It is about a man who turned his tenacious mind and undistracted gaze upon that body of water and decided that he would clean it up, and who, in the process, became somebody he never dreamed of being. The story is about the creation of a group of advocates in a part of the United States that had not known environmental advocacy, and a litany of successes that built an environmental ethic and caused this deeply beloved sedimentary river to run cleaner out of Georgia, into the sea.

The story is one of the transformation that is possible if one wakes up to the beauty and wonder of the earth, if one fears not, if one follows the path of his or her heart. The story of the transformation possible if people join together and decide to protect something they love. With love, many things are possible.

∽ In a boat at the mouth of the Altamaha River sat James Holland, around him the sea boiling, an eight-foot tide meeting thousands of gallons of fresh water minute by minute. The air was diaphanous with salty mist, like a veil. A finger of white sand reached out from Little St. Simons Island as if to calm the waters, and on that arm of firmament crowded ruddy turnstones, yellowlegs, oystercatchers, and willets.

Below, in the calmness and silence of the gray depths, a male blue crab carried his girl. She had molted and they had mated and for forty-eight hours he was carrying her, right-side-up and forward, and when her shell hardened he would release her, and she would begin her migration back into the salt, beautiful swimmer, with a cargo of two million eggs.

Many of which, for some reason, would not survive.

The boat carried Holland, like the river water carries nutrients to feed the plankton. Like the ocean carries salt. Holland was working these waters, motoring in his old boat from float to float he recognized so well. Every trip was a connect-the-dots; he hauled up the traps and took from them the crabs he was allowed to take, returning the rest to forage through the delta mud.

The numbers in the coolers spoke: they were falling, 300 pounds, 225, 175. Every year they fell—he remembers 1,500 pounds easily from one hundred traps in a day.

When Holland got hungry, he cut the engine and rested on the waters, dolphins in the foreground, pelicans diving headfirst, waves tapping the craft in a kind of SOS. "Do you see what is happening?" they were saying in their insistent language. The sky ever changed. The estuary stretched from the river, its bed a channel, a tablet upon which the water records what is happening to Georgia, from the first bubbles of spring water in the piedmont, to the confluence, to the fanned-out delta. On the other side of Holland lay the wide and faltering ocean.

Holland had no idea that his life was about to change permanently and that for the rest of his days he would become a voice for wild places and wild things. In a way this was a natural progression. Holland had been a warrior before, a marine, and he knew how to fight.

Like the spark of life the female blue crab carries in her orange sponge, an idea began in him. The voice of the voiceless spoke, and sitting in the rocking boat, eating a tuna sandwich, drinking warm coffee, he began to listen. *Willet, willet, willet*, the voice said. To watch it simply vanish is a sin against God.

Get up, James, the voice said. *The sun is already high in the sky. Stand up.*

You are a big man, you are strong, you have two hands capable of doing anything. You have a great mind. I have given you eyes to see and ears to hear. But I have given you something more, James, something special. What

I have given you is a heart big enough to care, with room enough to love
even the blue crab, which every day you hold in your big hands and admire.

When he reached land and stood up, the ground trembled.

    ☙ In the 1940s, a little boy who did not understand much of
what was happening in his world retreated to a creek near Cochran,
Georgia, to sail leaf boats, to build dams, to swim, and to fish. That
was James Holland. He will not talk much about what happened to
this little boy, because some of it he would rather forget. The river
was with him from the start.

Years later, after a career in the Marines and another in food ser-
vices, after a family was mostly raised and gone, after twenty-five
years in a boat in the hot sun, healing from all that had happened,
laboring to forget, drawing up traps, worrying some about money, he
came home to the river that knew him when he was a boy, lost and
found. The river found him, and then he returned and found it.

First there was a language to learn that had not been his own. It
was not "sook," not "gas line," not "Doboy Sound," not "robust red-
horse." This new language had long, scientific, technical, academic,
political words, and lots of initials. DNR, EPD, PSP, OVC, SMZ, MOA,
BMP. He had to learn it all, he who had never had a chance to go to
college, who had known nothing except hard work all his life.

By God, he would understand what the people who had the river
by the throat were saying. He learned more than he ever thought
possible. He could have been a biologist. He could have been a
lawyer. He could have been a writer. He could have been a public
official.

But James Holland was needed on the ground, on the water. He
was needed in public meetings, standing in front of the people.

Poor people live up and down this river. We work for years to buy
a johnboat. Some of us are badly educated, even ignorant. We throw
car tires and deer carcasses in the creeks. We dump trash and other
bad stuff in. We cut down trees.

But if we could understand a car engine, we could understand a river system, and for it to run it needs all its parts, and the parts have to be clean, in good working order, and they need fuel.

We needed to know how to translate all this.

Industry takes advantage of our ignorance, our silence, our consuming worries. It takes the fish, it takes the forests, it dumps copper and arsenic into the water, it erects coal plants that fill the air with mercury that drifts down into the river. It tries to build poultry processing plants, it schemes waste incinerators and biomass plants.

☙ In a poor region of the country, with a citizenry poorly educated about the environment, the river's time had come. Altamaha Riverkeeper was born, and Holland became the first actual, official Riverkeeper. Membership grew exponentially. The years passed and Holland traveled through the watershed, ferreting out lawlessness, ringing the bells of the people supposed to be regulating and protecting the watershed. There was a lawsuit, another lawsuit, another lawsuit. The federal judges were sympathetic to the law.

I've seen lots of activists at work and I've never seen anybody mobilize people the way Holland did. Maybe it's that he's clear about what he wants and he demands it. One thing I've noticed: he makes a lot of phone calls. Even when he could do a task alone with less effort, he takes time to involve people on many levels. He reaches out to people through their established friends. He worries with a problem until he has an idea. He finds someone who can help him. He asks for help. If he's told no, he asks again or finds someone else.

At 8:30 one Sunday morning many years ago, for example, my phone rang. "Were you sleeping?" Holland boomed.

"No," I said. "I was lying in bed, reading."

"I was laying in bed at 4:00 a.m. this morning, waiting until I could get to work," he said.

"You're crabbing today?"

"Yep," he said. "Heading out now. But listen, I have a favor. I just talked to my first cousin. Her husband is a professor in Athens. Which shows that all my folks didn't turn out like me. She'll get our press release to the university newspaper. I want you to mail it to her."

"OK," I said, and jotted down the address.

"And include a short note," said Holland, "to let my cousin know that a human being sent it."

A lot got done in ten years. Holland was out front, but behind him was Deborah Sheppard, the staunch and steady executive director who had left an Atlanta activist career to live on the coast, writing grants and press releases and doing the thankless work of keeping the whole ship afloat. She filled in Holland's gaps. She backed him up. They were a dynamic duo.

After a few years I began to notice something. In addition to the photos of destruction that Holland would send by e-mail, copying everybody he thought might help on every travesty, he began to e-mail pictures of beautiful things, wild things, rare things, endangered things: tiger swallowtail butterflies, wood storks constructing nests, raccoons washing food, water hyacinth, gulf frittillaries, sparring bucks, roseate spoonbills, sunning alligators, four wood ducklings on a log. As the years passed, the photos became more beautiful and more numerous. In the end, I think, the travesty was too much even for Holland's calm, rational, Marine-trained mind, too much for his immensely capacious heart. He couldn't keep focusing on tragedies.

"Even when I was seeing the degradation, I saw that beauty was still there," he said. "I found out that the most beautiful flowers on God's earth are around wetlands."

༈ After ten years, Holland retired. On his last official day on the job, in May of 2010, he called to tell me that the City of Jesup was dumping raw sewage again, the mess visible around the pipe, stringing in the trees. *There were more condoms than you can believe*, he said. *Every year they do it*, he said. *We talk to them and talk to them and they keep doing it.*

For his retirement, people came from up and down the river, from within the watershed and without, to honor him, and to thank him. They came from Tattnall County, Appling County, Wayne County, Toombs, Jeff Davis, McIntosh, Telfair. They came from Atlanta, Savannah, Macon, Athens. They thanked him for being a champion of rivers, conqueror of polluters and destroyers, defender of wild things, campaigner for justice.

"What you gave us was hope," I told him. "You made us want to fight. You were a warrior and you were fighting and we fell in step beside you. You inspired us. You performed miracles in front of our eyes."

From Holland I learned that transformation is possible. Watching him was watching the monarch emerge from her cocoon and take off over the tips of the milkweed.

Holland gave the Altamaha River a fighting chance. He gave it and its people the greatest gift a person could give, life itself, through eleven years of ceaseless labor and unflinching dedication to a grand corner of creation that is the Altamaha watershed.

Holland was the first Riverkeeper. But not the last. He simply started it all. It is a movement that is unstoppable.

Success is hard to measure. But I believe that water quality in the basin has improved steadily, incrementally, one part per million at a time, since Altamaha Riverkeeper lodged like a grain of sand in a clam and grew to become a pearl.

CHAPTER 4 *Seeking a Mission*

I.

Nothing here says de Soto.

Everything here says clear-cut. It says logging trucks. Pine plantation. The scrubby coinage of first growth.

Except to Dennis Blanton.

Dennis can see Spaniards across the river, which used to be right there, where the slough is now, dropping ten or twelve feet from the bedded rows of slash pine. That is the old run of the river, no doubt, but the river has fled, and in its place is a depression that sometimes fills with black water swirling beneath the feet of water striders.

The river, now, is a mile away.

But there *was* a river right there, and the tupelo, which didn't get cut in the season of cutting, are darkly and largely beautiful. It's the time of year, late summer, when golden orb and banana and crab spiders string tight cords through the trees, tying it all back together.

Dennis is watching the Spaniards, near six hundred of them, especially the one guy who seems to be telling everybody what to do, and he is watching the two hundred horses that raise a storm of dust, the hogs they attempt to keep from drifting, and the tired people in chains, trying to rest. He sees one of the restless band, a guide or interpreter, separate and step into the river. The man begins swimming with his feet, holding out of the water a bundle.

The man is native. He swims across and steps onto the bank we now stand on, water streaming from him. He knows he is in a friendly place. No one has attacked.

I am the son of the sun, his commander had said. *I am here to explore and claim your land.*

Dennis perceives behind us a large rectangular council house, its thatched roof supported by four giant timbers and at its center a hearth more than six feet in diameter, where a perpetual fire burns. The flames die only for the Green Corn Ceremony. Above the hearth, which is separated from the council house by wattle-and-daub partitions, the roof has been left open to create a smoke hole, and the surrounding thatch has also been plastered with a patina of clay. Around the lodge is a moat, a ditch, and in parts of it are tossed the remains of feasts.

In this feasting dump are hickory shells; the bones of passenger pigeon, whitetail deer, black bear, turkey, gopher tortoise, and raccoon; mussel shells; carapaces of box turtles, lamb's quarter seed, corn cobs.

Around the council house are dwellings.

Dennis sees all this. What I see is a clearing in a cutover forest. I see some sweet gums, and on the ground, among the weeds, passion vine and sassafras. I see Dennis, handsome archaeologist, a fire burning in his sky-blue eyes. When the fire is out, there is a faraway look.

∿ Back in high school in Alma, Georgia, in the 1970s, Dennis Blanton heard about a Spanish mission called Santa Isabel de Utinahica, established inland sometime during the early Spanish occupation, the mission period, of what is now Georgia. One day after he became an archaeologist, he took interest in finding it. He contacted his old friend Frankie Snow.

Frankie is a naturalist and a math and science professor at South Georgia College. His passion is archaeology. For decades, on his own time and with no assistance, Frankie has evaluated and mapped dozens of native sites. He has studied native pottery, putting entire broken vases and bowls back together, re-creating their etched designs on paper. Not only is he a friend of mine, he's a hero.

He's a quiet, unassuming man who isn't looking for attention. He's simply following a desire in his heart, which is to understand the life of the native people of southern Georgia.

Dennis called Frankie. "Frankie, you know this place like you know your own handwriting. I need your help. Where would you look for Santa Isabel de Utinahica?"

So Frankie took Dennis to a few spots.

One was a tract of land on the Ocmulgee River, near Horse Creek, long owned by the Glass family, which the cutting and bedding had exposed. There a solitary piece of early Spanish pottery had been discovered. The native materials found there were of the right timeframe.

With the gracious permission of owners Pat Glass Thorpe and Wilson Thorpe, in the summer of 2006 Dennis started digging. That year he had a field school consisting of a bunch of volunteers, including high school students from Atlanta, on the screens. Everybody was revved for Spanish artifacts, but they weren't finding anything. Nothing. Just dirt and roots and sand. Then one student called to Dennis, "Is this anything?"

In her palm was a glass bead.

Dennis was so excited he could barely speak. He knew this type bead. It was old old old, made early in the sixteenth century in Murano, Italy, brought to America by explorers specifically for use in trading with the natives.

By the end of the field season, they had found a single metal artifact, which also dated to the early sixteenth century.

Three explanations were possible. One, this was the village of native people who had indirect encounters with Spaniards. Two, this was the site of a short-term encampment of early Spanish explorers. Or three, this was a deserter residence.

Dennis dug at related sites in the area, then returned to the place that had produced the earlier artifacts. For four summers Dennis has dug. "Every time, we find Spanish stuff," he says, "and it's early."

What kinds of things?

Simple iron tools, chisels and flat wedges, glass beads, chains, sheet brass objects, an iron celt blade, a decorated iron awl, lead shot and chunk, lead nails, a silver pendant—items used for trading. Disk-shaped beads and a five-hundred-year-old ear bob, along with lots and lots of native pottery sherds and whelk artifacts.

"We've found the largest collection of early Spanish objects in the interior Southeast," Dennis says.

When Hernando de Soto came through Georgia in the spring of 1540, he took a meandering course. He had landed in Tampa Bay in June or July of 1539 and had spent the winter bivouacked in Tallahassee, four or five months, at what is called the Governor Martin site. Sometime in early spring he headed north, looking for precious metal. Gold.

Archaeologists have long drawn de Soto's route as a line from present-day Bainbridge to Augusta, generally speaking. De Soto arrived at the Savannah River in late April, looking for a native town he'd heard might have gold. These details are gleaned from his published journals. But no solid, compelling evidence, as Dennis puts it, has been found to support an exact route. "The strongest consensus is that he crossed the Savannah sometime soon after April 17," said Dennis, "and reached the legendary Indian capital of Cofitachequi— now in central South Carolina—later in the month, having crossed a depopulated 'wilderness' after departing the rich Georgia territories."

The day is sweltering hot when I visit the Glass site and meet Dennis for the first time. He is prematurely gray. He's wearing high-top boots, shorts, and a T-shirt whose blue-gray matches his eyes. The temperature hovers between 97 and 99, and a breeze that trails through now and then is the only relief. We stand in the shade, sweating.

"You think that de Soto came through here."

"I do," Dennis says, as convinced as if he's getting married.

He continues. "You know the quote, 'An army travels on its stomach.' The MO of the Spaniards was to connect the dots for food, intelligence, and company. They showed up prepared to do business with the natives. They were relieved to be greeted well by the chief of this territory. The natives were 'peaceful.' I believe the whole place was one big encampment."

"How long were they here?" I ask.

"I think de Soto was here for three days."

"So we'll have to redraw de Soto's route?"

"We've got to get de Soto from the Flint to the Little Ocmulgee."

❧   The Glass site is a little chopped-up place in the floodplain of the Ocmulgee, in one of the most rural and depopulated parts of Georgia. The dig is under blue tarp. Dennis stands at the edge and points out the hearth, the ditch, the feasting dump.

"When you were digging," I ask, "how did you know you'd found a hearth?"

"There were lots of signs," he says. "There were ashes and char. The sand below was bright orange, discolored from the heat."

I try to picture it.

"The most frustrating thing," says Dennis, "is that what it was like is hard to imagine. But that doesn't mean anything. Only that it's hard to imagine."

This was an edifice in the Indian world, he says.

This was a church, a courthouse.

This thing is Georgia's version of Pompeii.

You don't have to go far to hear stories of people from a long time ago, he says. They're right here.

Take this relatively small part of the country here, the so-called Big Bend of the Ocmulgee, he says, here you have every era. There's a microcosm of the entire human experience on a couple thousand acres.

This part of Georgia has as good a story as anywhere, he says. It's just been neglected.

II.

I had gone to Dennis to find out about native history along the main trunk of the Altamaha, and I had ended up with de Soto on the Ocmulgee, which *is* one of its main tributaries.

"The Altamaha is still terra incognita, archaeologically speaking," said Dennis. "We can tell you a whole lot more about the Altamaha before the year 1300 than after 1300."

"There was plenty of human activity in and around the Altamaha over the span of human time," he said. "It started as early as thirteen thousand years ago. But, for some reason, native populations became very sparse along the main stem of the river between about AD 1350 and 1700." As Dennis described it, the Altamaha corridor enjoyed popularity, then came some sort of dark ages that nobody yet understands. He knows this because the Spanish were explorers and missionaries who set up missions to congregate the Indians. When the Spaniards moved inland from the Georgia coast, in the 1600s, the Altamaha was an artery of indigenous travel. "The Spaniards had to follow the full stem of the Altamaha before they found people," said Dennis. "It was a virtual desert."

"This is not to say there was no activity whatsoever, but only that it was a low-level presence. People were present in greater numbers along the coast, and at and above the Forks." The Glass site is one such example. "Below the Forks we do not know of any significant native community occupied in the sixteenth century," said Dennis. "The Altamaha was a place of events, moments in history, short lived. But it was not a population center."

An exception was Sansavilla Bluff, where a temporary residence of mission Indians, mainly those who began to migrate from the lower Ocmulgee toward the coast under the influence of Spanish mission policy, was built. Otherwise, Altamaha proper was a relative dead zone.

III.

Still, plenty of native sites and evidence of native cultures, whatever the era, exist up and down the Altamaha. No more than a week ago, near a bridge that spans the river, my now teenage nephew, Carlin, found an old shoe polish bottle with WHITTEMORE spelled down its side. A foot away he found a wooden lure, still painted orange, circa 1940s. But the biggest find of his lucky day was the largest sherd of native pottery I've ever seen in the woods. Taking it from its resting spot was illegal, but we knew in our hearts it would be safer with us.

Besides, we wanted to get it to Frankie and show him the exact location it came from, an old riverbank.

I walk my dirt road down to our mailbox on Old River Road in Tattnall County and find chunks of flint, which can only be evidence of native habitation or visitation and for which the nearest source is up near Hawkinsville, on the Ocmulgee.

Maybe there were no native towns on the main stem of the Altamaha. Maybe there were no missions. Maybe de Soto went across instead of down.

But the natives lived here, long before we did, and before the likes of de Soto, and with a whole lot more digging we will unearth some of what they knew.

CHAPTER 5 *The Malacologists*

Today I am looking for mussels.

Looking involves crawling around in shallow water on hands and knees, feeling in the obscurity for hard, clamlike shells protruding from mud.

It is July 2000 and I am spending a day on the river with Dr. Eugene Keferl, a tall, lanky professor at Coastal Georgia Community College in Brunswick (now retired) and an expert in freshwater mussels. He calls the creatures unionids, also fluviatile mollusks. We are near Lane's Bridge, at a mussel bed that Dr. Keferl has studied for a long time. Intermittently one of us pulls a mussel to light. He lifts a big one, stares at it a minute, then tosses it back into the river. *Thonk.*

"Pocketbook," he says.

Dr. Keferl is not yet crawling. He moves a few steps and kneels again.

I hand him one I've found. He takes it, adjusts his glasses, then hands it back.

"Pocketbook," he says. The mussel is as large as a baseball and shaped something like a pita sandwich. It is black, shining pearly in places the black has worn away.

Dr. Keferl pulls up another mussel. "This is a lance," he says. It's long and narrow, like an antique case for spectacles.

Dr. Keferl examines the mussels we find, some for longer than others, and then we throw them back, until I have learned the common ones. Then I can inspect them and throw them back myself.

I want to find a spiny. Spinys used to be common, many decades ago. But those days of abundance are long gone. Finding one isn't impossible, only improbable. When I find it, the spiny mussel will be the typical clam shape, rounded, but with inch-long protrusions from the knob of its shell, like a calcified sea anemone.

"You need good healthy fish fauna to have good healthy mussel fauna," Dr. Keferl says.

"Why is that?" I ask.

"The life cycle of a mussel includes a parasitic stage, during which they attach to the fins or gills of fish, usually a particular fish."

"Each species has its preferred fish?"

"Basically. The mussel parasite drops off in ten to twenty days to burrow in the river sand and begin its mussel life."

"What host do the spinys need?"

"Well, that's a question we haven't yet answered," says Dr. Keferl.

The fish fauna are not so good in the river. With the introduction of flathead catfish, big cats have almost taken over. (The flatheads have been accepted by many sportfishers as a viable fishery. If you have nothing else, I suppose you embrace what you have. Restoration biologists have curtailed efforts to rid the river of them. In June 2006 a new record was set for a flathead, eighty-three pounds. It took twenty minutes to land the fish.)

Because of blank pages in the spiny mussel's natural history, scientists can't pinpoint the reason for its decline. Perhaps it is tied to a certain fish, which is also in decline, although a piscine host is not the only factor involved.

"Their habitat is stable banks," Dr. Keferl says. "They need stability. They don't like tree cutting, stump pulling, ditching. A lot are found in sloughs, backwaters."

"Their future looks bleak," I say.

"The spiny may be headed toward extinction, I'm afraid," says Dr. Keferl.

~ I was introduced to Dr. Keferl's work at a technical meeting conducted in the summer of 1999 by The Nature Conservancy (TNC). Dr. Keferl, a poised man with a shock of graying hair, talked about the distribution and abundance of his beloved fluviatile mollusks.

About three hundred species of freshwater mussels are documented in the mainland United States. The eastern United States boasts the best freshwater mussel populations in the world. The Tennessee River system, before it was dammed, won top prize for most diversity and abundance.

Eighty percent of freshwater mussel species, or 270 of them, live in the Southeast. Soberingly, however, 70 percent of southeastern species are threatened, endangered, or extinct. Let's say it without the numbers—the Southeast is the most biologically rich and imperiled region for freshwater species.

"More than two-thirds of US freshwater mussels are extinct or at risk of extinction," wrote zoologist Lawrence Master, author of TNC's report "Rivers of Life: Critical Watersheds for Protecting Freshwater Biodiversity." One in nine mussel species went extinct in the twentieth century.

Of those mussels found in Georgia, twenty-five species are endangered, thirteen are threatened, and thirteen are of special concern.

A beautiful mussel taxonomy is found in the Altamaha. It includes:

Altamaha arc mussel (*Alasmidonta arcula*)
Barrel floater (*Anodonta couperiana*)
Georgia elephant ear (*Elliptio dariensis*)
Altamaha slabshell (*Elliptio hopetonensis*)
Variable spike (*Elliptio icterina*)
Altamaha lance (*Elliptio shepardiana*)
Altamaha spiny mussel (*Elliptio spinosa*)
Altamaha pocketbook (*Lampsilis dolabraeformis*)
Rayed pink fatmucket (*Lampsilis splendida*)
Inflated floater (*Pyganodon gibbosa*)
Savannah lilliput (*Toxolasma pullus*)
Eastern creekshell (*Villosa delumbis*)

Ten years ago, malacologists believed that seven species were endemic to the river, found *only* in the watershed. These were arc mussel, Georgia elephant ear, Altamaha slabshell, Altamaha lance, Altamaha spiny mussel, Altamaha pocketbook, and the rayed pink fatmucket. But research has been correcting that science, as I have come to learn.

⟳   An angler approaches Dr. Keferl and me. Apparently he doesn't dare come any closer than forty feet to the two grown, sensible-looking people creeping around in the water on hands and knees, fully clothed, soaking wet.

"Whatcha doing?" the fisher asks, without prelude. I guess we look as if we've lost something. Which we have.

Dr. Keferl says nothing so I take it upon myself to ease the poor bugger's mind.

"Looking for mussels."

"Muscles? That's something you develop, not find."

"Not that kind."

"Oh," he grins.

"Looks like a clam. But bigger. There used to be a lot of them in this river, but they're on the decline. They don't like pollution. We're looking at what's left."

"Can you eat them?"

"Not recommended. Some people have and they've wound up pretty sick. I think Native Americans ate them, but the water quality was a lot better then. Is this your favorite spot?"

"Pretty much. I better get at it."

"Well, that's your ecology lesson for today."

He tips his hand and pulls the trolling motor.

⟳   On this July day, Dr. Keferl and I find many kinds of mussels but not a spiny. We don't even find an empty shell.

The naturalist Milton Hopkins, who became a mentor and friend, and with whom I corresponded regularly for over a decade, told me that, besides the spiny, other freshwater mussels are no longer found in area rivers. The bank climber. The three rib. In House Creek, over near Fitzgerald, he used to find mussels with real pearls inside. At least that's what he said. But in a letter Dr. Keferl wrote to Milton in

1997, he said, "I have looked at the insides of hundreds of mussels from the Altamaha River system and I have never found a pearl."

The decline of mussels is telling. Their importance lies chiefly in their being aquatic biomonitors, indicators of water quality and health. Habitat degradation is their main enemy. Mussels are particular about habitat.

Dams, for example, are hard on them. Dams increase sedimentation, reduce oxygen levels by choking flow, and either dry out mussel beds (below the impoundment) or inundate them (above).

Other degradations include discharges of effluent—wastewater treatment, industrial waste, waste from food processing plants—as well as industrial cooling water. Neither do mussels like eutrophication, which is nutrient overloading—including elevated phosphorus and nitrogen from fertilizer runoff or any point-source pollution—that stimulates plant growth and leads to a dearth of oxygen. Mussels don't do well in low-oxygen conditions, which can be caused by concentrations of carbon dioxide and decomposition by bacteria. In the Altamaha, mussels have disappeared from the waters downstream of the paper mill run by Rayonier at Jesup.

Freshwater mussels don't tolerate salinity either. Lewis Island is as far coastward as Dr. Keferl has found living mussels, he says. (Bartram, however, was believed to have discussed the spiny mussel from the vicinity of "Frederika," but whether or not he meant Fort Frederica, on the coast, is unclear.)

༄ An hour later we're at a new sandbar and find ourselves again near the same angler. He's fishing now.

"What you fishing for?" I call.

"Mullet."

"Will they take a hook?"

"Like it's candy."

"I've only seen them netted. What's the bait?"

"Worms."

"Regular earthworms?"

"Plain ole earthworms."

"That's all you have to do?"

"I attract them with salt."

"How salt?"

"I hang a sack or a block of salt off the boat. That brings them up."

"They think it's a little bit of ocean?"

"I guess."

"Never heard of that. I'd like to try it. Good luck catching them."

"That's your fishing lesson for today!" he calls.

Bird List While Mussel Hunting:
great egret, snowy egret, great blue heron, little blue heron,
yellow-billed cuckoo, wood stork, osprey, red-shouldered hawk,
turkey buzzard, white ibis, kingfisher, and at the end of the day,
three swallow-tailed kites come to examine our activities,
wheeling over the floodplain.

Ten years later, in the summer of 2010, I spend a splendid morning on the river with DNR malacologist Jason Wisniewski, who I will learn is nicknamed Wiz. Jason is from a holler in western Pennsylvania, an hour out of Pittsburgh, coal country. That he is an Appalachian kid is evidenced in his accent. He began his studies in fisheries biology, thinking to work with introduced trout or reservoirs, until a malacologist at Tennessee Tech, where he was a student, offered him employment. "I like iss," he thought. That's the way he talks.

"So mussels kind of found me," he says.

Raven happily takes the morning off from endless farm chores and accompanies us mussel hunting. We meet Jason at a dust-clouded convenience store off Highway 169 between Glennville and Jesup, and follow him to Upper Wayne Landing, which, like most landings on the river, is not easily found, reached by a maze of river roads. We admit embarrassment that a kid from Pennsylvania knows the roads better than we, who live thirty minutes away. The landing has been updated, with a newly concreted slope to the chartreuse water and a grotesquely supersized parking lot. It has a little shelter for picnics and a kiosk with a sign that reads "Loaner Vests for Children" above a set of empty hooks. Apparently this part of south Georgia is not ready for communal sharing.

Jason is a big guy, tall and strong. He used to be a lot bigger, he says. A grim cardiology report convinced him to stop drinking Mountain Dew, and in the last six months he's lost fifty pounds. Neither his goatee nor sunglasses in any way hide the openness in Jason's face. He smiles a lot.

Jason is accompanied by a graduate technician, Mieko Camp, a short, pretty, and capable woman who graduated high school in Ocilla and is headed toward a PhD. Jason's lively, black-and-white-pied dog, Duke, is also along.

Jason and Mieko shuck off a layer of their uniforms and pull on thermalwear—preparation for long hours in water—and dive shoes. Jason slaps on a white cowboy hat and straps a dive knife to his leg. Raven and I wait, dressed in tatty, long-sleeved work clothes.

Jason and Mieko launch a dull-green skiff, and we clamber in and motor upriver, four people and a dog in a flat-bottom boat.

If I were dropped out of the sky onto this boat, I would hope to know my river. This river is wide, a width that's hard to describe because it varies from place to place and from season to season, sometimes as wide as a football field is long and sometimes as wide as it is narrow, and sometimes it is wider than my town, Reidsville. The river is deep and obviously powerful, so that to look at it one immediately feels humbled. At first gaze one checks for a life preserver. This is a river that doesn't take no for an answer.

I would hope to know my river from the Mississippi if I parachuted down blindfolded onto it. I would want to distill its essence, and distinguish it from the Hudson, or the Amazon, or the Nile. I would hope to be able to recognize it as home.

The water is a strange shade of greenish yellow-brown. It's the color of liquid silt, of unbleached paper, of certain large locusts. Each bank is a wall of trees, sometimes scattered beneath with cypress knees, broken occasionally by a wheat-colored sandbar or a cutbank.

We cruise to the mouth of a slough. Jason approaches a muddy apron of land, littered with humus, and stalls the motor at a break in black willows. Mieko throws an anchor on the bank—she's strong for a small woman. When she leaps out she sinks to her calves. She deftly disentangles herself from the mire and tugs the boat toward land.

"I thought we'd look here for the Altamaha arc," Jason says. "For a long time we thought the arc mussel was rare. Then in October 2008 we made the single biggest collection in years. Forty-six mussels were found, tagged, and returned to the river in twenty-nine person-hours. Since then, we have collected at the site several additional times and found quite a few more untagged arc mussels, suggesting that there is quite a substantial population present at the site." He cuts the motor and gets out in knee-deep water.

"Mussels like gently sloping banks that are stable," Jason says. "They like really fine sand, packed hard, so that when high water is coming down they're not washed away."

Today, here, the river's streamflow is at 3,000 cubic feet per second, normal for summer. That translates to 22,441 gallons. In April 2009 the river topped out at 100,000 cubic feet per second, which means 748,000 gallons, historically high water levels. If that wasn't the record, it was close. "It was a real channel-forming event," Jason says. "This place stayed the same."

We tumble out into the water. I tolerate colder baths at home. Slowly, without it seeming like work at all, but as if four friends are hanging out in a river, laughing at the dog, we plunk ourselves in the shallows, sitting on the bottom, water to our chests, feeling lazily around us. Mussels bury themselves partway in sand, where they open their shells and filter micronutrients. They're easy to find by running hands along the bottom and gently pulling them out.

You know how people fiddle with things when they talk? They pluck grass stems or run sand through their fingers. That's what we are doing, fiddling underwater.

Jason has a calm, lackadaisical way about him. Because the water is murky, what we see of him appears to be relaxing, cooling off. He patiently allows the morning to unfold, without control. I touch a mussel and dig it up.

"That's an *Elliptio hopetonensis*," Jason says. A slabshell that he calls the Hope. He begins to point out its particularities—a bulge here, a ridge there. Nothing about Jason is rushed.

I memorize the shape of the Hope. My short-term memory is good.

"This one, see, is different." Jason has a mussel in his hand, as if he flicked a magic wand and a mussel appeared. Abracadabra. "The shape is still flattened, but more angular. This is *Elliptio dariensis*. Elephant ear."

I memorize it too. Next I pull up a lance.

With each mussel, Jason patiently points out differences, similarities. One was a young version of another; one was male, one female. Jason, it seems, has made himself my personal tutor for the morning. A cowboy magician tutor.

He explains how the mussel-fish connection works: A male mussel looses his gametes into the current above a female mussel. She opens her shell and collects them. When it's time to release her fertilized eggs, she opens her shell and reels out a lure that mimics a small fish. This flaps and flashes in the current. When a fish approaches, thinking to eat it, she sprays her eggs in his face. They attach to scales and gills, where, for some reason, they stay for a few weeks. This part is little understood. Are they after a chemical found in the fish's blood? Mussel eggs have been cultured on blood samples in the laboratory, so that makes sense. But what chemical? And why?

Now Raven is on his knees, feeling around in the water. The first mussel he brings up is very small, like tortellini.

"That's the little invasive exotic," I say. "Corbicula?"

"Yes," Jason says. I could learn a lot from his patience.

"They seem to proliferate even as the natives decline," I say.

"They're everywhere," Raven says.

"They found the right conditions," says Jason.

Raven hurls a few handfuls, futilely, on the bank. The dog thinks it is a game of fetch and darts up to retrieve them. Out in the current something large splashes—on the Altamaha, a smart first thought is always gator.

"Sturgeon," says Jason.

"Did you see it?" I ask.

"No," he says. "But I could tell by the sound. But don't think alligators aren't here." Then he tells the story of his first time diving in the river, in very dim water, of course. He felt something strange right beside him, on the river bottom, something with deep ridges. "Hmmmm," he thought. He moved his hand and felt again. This time he was feeling a tail. "That's an alligator," he thought, scared silly. He eased away and went up for air.

"It was a big one too," he says. Since then, not being afraid hasn't been easy.

When the story ends, a more unusual mussel materializes in Jason's hand. Open sesame!

"This is a pocketbook," he says. "A female."

"How can you tell?" I ask.

"By the curve on this end," he says, demonstrating.

Not only are the corbiculas everywhere, so are the native species. I'm no scientist, so it's hard to be certain, but the mussels seem more abundant than they were a decade ago. Maybe Altamaha Riverkeeper, TNC, and the DNR are accomplishing something.

"Gosh, I'm finding tons of mussels," I say. "Should I collect them?"

Jason says yes, and Mieko hands Raven and me each a mesh bag. We don't ask which species Jason needs for his studies. We simply gather mussels.

Give me something to collect and I'm your woman. The gatherer instinct is strong. The bag rapidly fills.

Really I was looking for the spiny. Each hard shell on the river floor excited me, but what I wanted to feel were the long rays of a spiny's spines. I'd never found one, and I thought that would be good, finding a spiny once in my life. Like holding an indigo or seeing a sturgeon at the apex of its jump.

Once at a reading at Emory University in Atlanta a young man came up to me. "I don't know if you have one of these yet," he said, holding out his hand. In it was the shell of a spiny mussel. The only other one I'd seen had been in the collection of Milton Hopkins, my naturalist friend and the author of *In One Place: The Natural History of a Georgia Farmer*, and I was flooded with mental images of Milton, who had very recently died.

"Where did you get this?" I said, excited.

"I've been studying mussels on the Altamaha," he said. "I'm writing my thesis on them."

"You found this one like this, right?"

He looked quizzical.

"Not alive," I said.

"Oh," he said. "It was dead. I found the shell."

I held the young man by both shoulders and told him that a spiny mussel shell was the best gift anyone could give me. I thanked him for being so thoughtful.

"I thought you'd like it," he said.

"What a rarity," I said.

I kept his card. Another Jason, last name Meador. He'd worked with Wiz.

"Spinys are around," the Jason I'm with now says. "Not very numerous or common. They're a candidate for endangered status. It's possible we could find one."

"Let's," I say.

Mussels are everywhere. I tug them out of the sand one after another. Pocketbook, slabshell, lance, lance, lance, slabshell, arc. Jason makes a rayed pink fatmucket turn up in his hands. It is an even stouter mussel than the pocketbook and is often a lovely peachy color with thin, brown, parallel bands running the length of its shell.

Before long Raven and I are lugging around small nets full of mussels. We are slow to realize that Jason and Mieko are not gathering. They are looking only for certain ones: the arc, a specimen of which Jason has by now found and shown us; and also mussels previously tagged, with tiny numbered placards glued to their shells, in order to follow movement and growth patterns.

What Jason is doing in the water is sifting mussels with his hands. He can tell without looking what species he touches, and the common ones he forsakes, bringing to air only the unusual ones.

Mieko is doing the same, except she is using a mask and snorkel, ranging farther from us, rising to the surface with a mussel or two stuffed in her wetsuit. To see them, she says, she has to swim with her eyes a few inches from the riverbottom.

I ask Jason to clarify which mussels are endemic. In the past decade, some of those once thought to be found only in the mainstem Altamaha have been found in other river systems. Now, those still thought endemic are three, the Altamaha spiny, Altamaha lance, and Georgia elephant ear. It appears that the Altamaha arc, Altamaha slabshell, Altamaha pocketbook, and inflated floater may occur in the Ogeechee and possibly Savannah basins, two rivers that run north of the Altamaha and also flow into the Atlantic.

We inch through the shallow water toward the black willows, from which alligators would by now be spooked, and then progress through the willows. The bar is extremely productive. When our mesh bags are full, we park them in shallow water and keep searching, my heart set on a spiny.

Any mussel in a damaged river is good, but a spiny is hope.

Toward lunchtime we hoist the bags onto the muddy strand and lay them out in rows. We have found seven species, and the numbers, even with only two of us collecting, are impressive—153 lance, 139 slabshell, 32 elephant ear, 10 variable spike, 6 rayed pink fatmucket, 9 pocketbook (4 already tagged), and 10 arc (5 tagged).

When it comes to the spiny, however, Jason's luck runs out. Try as he might, he can't make one appear. The magic show is over.

We lunch on boiled eggs, crackers, tuna, and pound cake on a spit of hard clean sand under a droop of black willows. At our feet the river, huge and brooding, hides from science all kinds of mysteries that the most curious among us want to know, *have* to know, work all our lives to know.

"Earth and ocean want their mysteries," wrote Linda Hogan. "It is not meant for light and human knowledge to shine into every unlit corner of the ocean, the earth, and the universe."

May enough of those mysteries be known and enough go forever undisclosed.

CHAPTER 6　*Under the Franklin Tree*

Another thing about the Altamaha makes it a very special river. That thing is a tree.

I would like to tell you that I took a walk in the woods and saw the Franklin tree.

But the tree no longer lives in the woods. In fact, over half a century ago a granite monument to it was erected off Highway 84 near Doctortown.

I had to go all the way to Philadelphia to see *Franklinia*—820 miles to see a tree native to the river that runs two miles from my home, a tree last seen in the wild in 1803.

    On October 1, 1765, John Bartram, a Quaker botanist traveling with his son William through the South, crossed the Altamaha River at Fort Barrington, above Darien, and rode horseback through a bottomland near the coast. The Bartrams were on a botanical expedition, collecting seeds and plants from the swamps and sandhills and prairies of the southeastern United States.

Bartram had just been appointed Royal Botanist for North America by King George III, which awarded him a fifty-pound annual stipend that allowed him to travel widely through the colonies looking for unusual specimens for his own gardens and for plantspeople in Europe. He ran a nursery and mail order business at his home on the Schuylkill River near Philadelphia. This home became America's first botanical garden, as he and his son introduced into cultivation more than two hundred native plants.

"This day we found several very curious shrubs," John wrote in his journal on that October day in 1765, "one bearing beautiful good fruite." By "fruite" John meant seedpods.

There is no record of the Bartrams collecting seeds that day. Perhaps they collected seeds that subsequently failed to germinate.

At any rate, eight years later, in 1773, son William, who would become more famous than his father, returned to the same location and found the tree in bloom. Now he was traveling under the patronage of a London physician. William wrote about the day in his book *Travels through North and South Carolina, Georgia, and Florida*, one of the first pieces of nature writing about the South: "On drawing near the fort I was greatly delighted at the appearance of two beautiful shrubs in all their blooming graces. One of them appeared to be a species of *Gordonia*, but the flowers are larger, and more fragrant than those of the *Gordonia lasianthus*."

William Bartram dubbed the tree *Gordonia pubescens* because it resembled the native loblolly bay (*Gordonia lasianthus*) and because its fruits were pubescent, or hairy. He sent a specimen to London and collected seeds from the plant, which he shipped back to Philadelphia, to his father. "We never saw it grow in any other place," he wrote, "nor have I ever seen it growing wild in all my travels."

Meanwhile, English botanists determined that the tree was a distinctive genus. The Bartrams named the new genus and species *Franklinia alatamaha*, after Ben Franklin, family friend, and in honor of the river on which the small tree grew.

The last sighting of the Franklin tree in the wild was in 1803 by John Lyon, a British plantsman. Subsequent searches were fruitless, and the plant is believed extinct in nature.

Nobody knows exactly why. Some blame a fungus. Some blame the flooding of the river. Some say *Franklinia* is an Asian tree, member of the tea family, brought on some ancient ship to the coast of Georgia and lost to encroaching woods the same way ornamentals at abandoned homesteads are lost. Some blame climate change.

In August of 2008, traveling south from a conference, my husband and I paused in Philadelphia to visit Bartram's Garden, where the Franklin tree is yet cultivated. We arrived just in time to catch the day's last tour of Bartram's stone house. The senior Bartram began building the lodging soon after he bought the property in 1728. It was finished in the 1740s.

Even in my hurry, I could not help noticing plants outside that are also growing in my yard, such as sweet shrub, unmistakable.

The tour guide was a frank and enthusiastic woman who, after years working there, still got excited about the house. *Here are some of William's botanical sketches. This was John's study. This is a map of old Philadelphia. This is a dried ox bladder, which would have been used to transport seeds. These floorboards are of chestnut, fourteen to fifteen inches wide. Fireplaces were used for heating.*

We were upstairs in the stone house built before our country was even a country, standing on floorboards planed from trees cut over 250 years prior, surrounded by historical artifacts from a time in which the pursuit of knowledge of the natural world was among the most noble of professions—surrounded by American history at its birthplace—when the guide pointed out the Franklin tree to me. There it was, out the window, growing near the house, in Bartram's Upper Garden, a tree lost to my place and thus to me, a tree that had its origins where I had mine.

It was a bright, beautiful tree about twenty feet tall, with lance-shaped, pea-green leaves and a trunk striped with vertical lines. Its shape was perfect.

And . . .

The tree was bedecked with white flowers the size of teacups. Blooming!

∽ Our entire trip had been touched by luck, and we were lucky twice that day. First, Mark Dion's exhibits were on display at the Bartram house. In late 2007 and early 2008, Dion, an artist, flea marketer, and cultural anthropologist, had retraced the journey of William Bartram. He had mailed back what he found, and later built curio cabinets to house his modern collections—part natural history, part cultural commentary, part art. Nothing escaped his scrutiny of this world remade, and his collections include shards of porcelain, shotgun shells, turtle shells, antique vials, deer moss, a peach pit, a bleach lid, a wine cork, and starfish, which is to say the heartbreaking mixture of industrial civilization and what's left of nature. One of Dion's cabinets was filled with hand-drawn postcards mailed to staff members. Another was crammed with packages that contained racist objects—belt buckles adorned with Confederate flags, the statuary of little black Sambo fishing, a Mammy saltshaker—found at flea markets, still sealed, never to be seen again by human eyes, I was told. Another contained a kitschy collection of plastic and glass alligators.

The second stroke of luck took place at the coach house, where Mary Fran Cardamore was hanging her art in preparation for the following day's opening of her show. Her work is botanical collage that incorporates mounted specimens, botanical illustrations, calligraphy, and found objects. "I got started with this when I began planting a native garden," she said to us, as she paused from measuring and hanging. "I am fascinated with horticulture, especially medicinal plants." Her mixed-media pieces bring to life the stories of plants, their life histories, folklore, ranges, and medicinal values.

Both artists intrigued me because I am fascinated by the idea of collections and how disparate elements are taken from native environments and put together to make a statement. For Dion, the statement was: Look at the junk I found—oh, here and there a treasure—in the footsteps of Bartram. And for Cardamore, the statement was: some people still love plants the way John and William did.

❧   I caught up with Joel Fry, curator, in the museum shop. He was a thin, outdoorsy man with longish hair in the early stages of graying.

"I don't understand why the Franklin tree went extinct in the wild," I said.

"What happened is still a giant mystery," Fry said. He offered an explanation for its demise. "Bartram probably saw a very old colony," he said. "Perhaps, like other plants, it had moved south with the ice ages. As the ice receded and the oceans rose, plants tended to re-migrate back again."

But the *Franklinia* doesn't self-seed well. It doesn't produce seed prolifically, and it requires over a year to mature its seed. A lot of its viable seeds don't get spread by birds. So, likely the species didn't evolve or migrate quickly enough to escape rising seas. Basically, *Franklinia* drowned.

Bartram's Garden is not the only place the tree can be found. Many botanical collections now contain *Franklinia alatamaha*. Arnold Arboretum of Harvard University has a specimen over a century old, planted in 1905. The plant is propagated and sold, and many individuals now grow them.

~ Later, I strolled through America's first botanical garden, where at its peak more than two thousand native and exotic plants grew. There I found bitternut hickory, hop hornbeam, Carolina silverbell, and Cornelian cherry dogwood. I marveled at a yellow-wood collected in Tennessee by André Michaux and sent to William Bartram. I gazed into the branches of a London plane tree. I touched the oldest ginkgo in North America, imported from England and given to William Bartram in 1785.

I walked with the ghosts of Ben Franklin, Thomas Jefferson, and George Washington, who had also visited, circling past museum shop and barn, along the river walk, past the site of Bartram's cider press, and then returning to the Upper Garden.

This is how I came to sit for a while beneath the Franklin tree.

Some of the blooms had already fallen to the ground and they lay wilted around me. Others, on the low branches, were yet open. Each of the three-inch-wide blooms consisted of five petals that led to a cluster of stamens orange as an oriole. The flowers smelled exactly like roses.

I had a wonderful rest beneath the Franklin tree.

CHAPTER 7 *Sandhills*

I am standing on a sandhill at Big Hammock Natural Area (closest town Glennville) with ecologist Lisa Crews, a redhead with nice glasses who manages to look stylish even in her DNR uniform. Today she is leading a cluster of botanists as well as botanist wannabes (Raven and me) on a walkabout of the sandhills.

We're standing at the bottom of Big Hammock, a sandhill forty-five to fifty feet high, a small mountain in the endless flatness of the coastal plain, where the ocean used to lap. But this is like no mountain you've seen. Here deep sand is carpeted with lichens, strange life-forms, growing beneath stunted and twisted trees. I have the feeling of being a Lilliputian.

Twenty thousand years ago the climate of southern Georgia was windy and dry, Lisa is telling us. Prevailing winds, 60 percent of them, came out of the southwest. During the glacial periods of the Pleistocene, as the coastal plain was exposed, these winds created a strange phenomenon—they crafted inland eolian dunes to the north and east of the Altamaha and other coastal floodplains.

The river, almost a mile away, is the last thing one thinks of while standing at the foot of this sandhill. Here the biota reminds me more of a desert.

These relict dunes, called riverine sandhills, scrub hammocks, or evergreen hammocks, are strange and magical environments. Charles Wharton, preeminent Georgia ecologist, used the word "fairyland." They are extremely rare formations, with unique soil and landforms. Although discontinuous, they contain species similar to barrier island sand dunes as well as the fall-line sandhills, which makes sense, since all were created from the same phenomenon of dry, raging winds.

"How could the sandhills have grown so big?" someone asks.

"We believe the river fifteen to thirty-thousand years ago had more braided channels, like an estuary," Lisa says. "More exposed sands, meaning not covered by vegetation, were available. The climate caused rapid changes from wet to dry, and winds swept the sands into piles here. And this is small comparatively. Some dunes on the Ohoopee, for example, are over one hundred feet high."

I'm going to give you some advice right away about botanists. Never go out in the woods with them. Never go anywhere. If you do, you'll never get to where you're going. They want to stop every few feet to bend down and look at something. They carry little magnifying glasses with them so they can count parts of flowers so small they'd get lost in a thimble. The botanists are shamelessly looking to see if leaves are hairy or smooth, if they have glands, how their veins run. You have to keep your body covered when you're with botanists.

So it's mid-October, a day that would win a beauty pageant it is so fine, a perfect day, and I'm standing at a granite-and-stone marker erected by the National Park Service in 1976 that proclaims this scrubby little hill a Registered National Landmark. And I'm with a group of people who have their pants tucked in their socks and who are crawling around in the grass with magnifying glasses. They are examining the grasses, in fact, and speaking a language I don't understand while doing so.

"I think these are *Aristida purpurascens*."

"Well, it could be three-awn grass. Looks like wiregrass but isn't."

"Oh, here's a little bluestem," someone calls. "Related to *Andropogon*."

Come on, people, you're embarrassing me. Somebody's gonna pass on the road and see me out here with you all, crawling around in the dirt. I live in this county, remember? Also, I want to see what's at the top of this little mountain, so we've got to pep it up a little.

"We've got *Vitis rotundifolia* all over the place."

"Here's *Smilax pumila*."

What, have we been invaded? This sounds a lot like *Star Wars* to me.

A few feet ahead is a flower in bloom. Don't give these people a flower. They go crazy.

"*Liatris*," one says.

"*Graminifolia*, I think," says another. "Oh dear, that genus has been broken into several. The problem is categorizing."

The problem is that getting up this fifty-foot hill is going to take all day at this rate. And step back, people. You're smothering that poor flower. Quit peering down its throat, trying to see its ovaries.

Lisa is trying to explain to us that the word "hammock" comes from the Spanish word *hamaca*, which may be how Jamaica got its name. A *hamaca* is a hill that has lush green vegetation rising from a flat landscape, in this case the ancient terraces of the Altamaha floodplain.

Just then someone screams. I run over, thinking they've found a mummy or something. Gold, maybe. "*Sorghastrum secundum!*" the guy says excitedly.

"What?" I say. I'm trying to see what the heck he's talking about.

"*Sorghastrum secundum!*" He points to a pathetic stalk of weed. I raise my eyebrows and he gets a sorrowful look on his face. "Lopsided Indian grass," he says, as if he's talking to a moron.

Which, in a way, he is.

For the next ten minutes everybody's crowded around this little stalk of grass talking about its hairs and glands and veins. I'm watching the road. I mean, botanists can look at a single plant for a very long time. People, I think I'll just sit over here by the monument and take a little nap while you count hairs. Wake me up when you want to see the mountaintop.

And so it goes, creeping up the hill. It's *Agalinis* and *Quercus* and *Pinus*.

The group of botanists is about a quarter of the way up the little sandhill when I realize that we're a circus out here. It's just one spectacle after another. I think about the circus because yesterday, it came to my hometown of Reidsville. It came in tractor trailers and travel trailers and parked on the ball field at the elementary school. By late afternoon it had erected a tall, pointy tent and a little corral where some ponies, some goats, and a camel were pooping on the turf.

Neither hell nor high water could keep me away from the circus. I have a trapeze in the galley at my house, and one of my favorite things to do is get up there and do some tricks. My husband insists that I drag a big mattress under the bar when I do this. I'm training the dogs too. I've got one of them, the black lab named Matilda, sitting, shaking with her left paw, shaking with her right paw, and lying down. Rolling over is next but she's not getting it, which gives me pause: how am I going to get her to jump through a flaming hoop?

At the circus, a man piled a bunch of chairs on top of each other on a table and climbed up and stood on his head. After he came down, a clown ran out and sold peanuts. A woman in a sequined, plumed, low-cut outfit a little too skin-tight for Reidsville went up high and turned upside-down, then hung by her feet, and then flew from one trapeze to another. After she came down, a clown ran out and sold cotton candy.

A guy popped out dressed like he'd been mucking out a barn, and he coerced goats into doing some tricks. I didn't know goats would jump and carry on like that. A pony did some high-stepping and weaving. The camel did some kneeling. Somebody showed off an alligator and then a boa constrictor, and for five bucks you could get a Polaroid picture of yourself taken with either the alligator or the snake. A couple of clowns acted like fools, then the trapeze artist went up again in another outfit made of ribbons. I was so excited I almost fell through the bleachers.

These botanists are as thrilled with the lowliest sandhill weeds, I realized, as I was with the clowns and the dancing goats.

Finally I know a plant. I almost don't see it for my big hat. It's gold-enrod and it's in bloom.

"But *which solidago*?" someone asks.

Which *solidago*?

"Looks like *odorata*," someone says. "Not *pauciflosculosa*."

Can somebody please tell me what's going on? Obviously all these people took Latin in high school and I didn't. *Hamamelis. Vaccinium. Cliftonia. Helianthus*. Have you ever heard words with more syllables? This is a foreign language for really smart people who understand the longest words in the world.

Finally they start translating for me. I get excited too, waiting for the next act.

"*Balduina angustifolia*. Honeycomb head."

"*Paronychia*. Nailwort. Same family as chickweed and carnations."

"*Lycopodiella*. Rabbit tobacco. *Carphephorus*. Deer tongue."

Finally I sneak around a bush and take out my hand lens, so I can see the hairs and stuff.

"What's this?" my husband asks.

"Oh, just a little magnifying glass I found in my backpack," I say.

"Hmmm," he says.

Pretty soon I'm peering at spiny bracts and pollen sacs, bending and kneeling and crawling.

At the top of the little hill, all joking aside, the world is a different place. Earth star and sand spikemoss and little round mosses called sandhill reindeer lichen plaster the ground. There are cacti. These grow around and underneath dwarfed and gnarled sand live oak, turkey oak, sand post oak, and myrtle oak. There is Darlington oak. There is witch hazel and sparkleberry and horse sugar. There is go-pher apple, growing at the perfect level for gopher tortoises. Many of these plants sport thick, leathery, or wooly leaves, special adaptations to a harsh environment.

We don't see any animals, but what might be there, were it not for the invasion, are burrowers, such as the gopher tortoise, as well as gopher frog, indigo snake, red-tailed skinks, armadillos, wolf spiders, and oak toads.

There is a grand finale in this funny circus of a day. It is the rarest of rare plants, *Elliotia racemosa*, a small deciduous tree that produces plume-shaped, showy white flowers in June and July. It was observed by William Bartram in 1773 somewhere near the Savannah River. After 1808, when Stephen Elliot collected it near Waynesboro, no wild populations came to light until Roland Harper, with Walter Hendricks, rediscovered it in 1901.

We all stand and applaud. The curtain falls and it's time to go home, take off my big boots, my big hat, and my red bandanna, extract my pant cuffs from my socks, and look for ticks.

"Have you ever seen smarter people?" my husband says on the way home.

"Never," I say. "Seriously. I wish I knew a fraction of what any one of them knows."

"I had a really good time," he says.

So did I. Better than a circus.

CHAPTER 8 *Blackberry Swamp*

Late May, blackberries were ripe in Moody Forest. I knew they were there. I was salivating at the thought of them.

Of all the public and accessible land along the Altamaha, the place I go most often is Moody Forest. It's the tract geographically closest and the one with which I'm most familiar.

Raven and I had noticed the Moody blackberries in early May, when we hiked with friends to see five-hundred-year-old cypress and tupelo. The blackberries were huge, big as blackberries of the Northwest. For two weeks we tried to go back, but you know how life is. There's always something, mostly work, calling you away from the world.

We live on a farm, so for us, work is usually good work. Time-consuming, yes, but good. Spring is busy with seed-starting and preparation for planting, with new hatchings of chicks and keets, and kidding or calving or lambing. We try to grow as much of our food as we can. And we like to gather what we can.

"The blackberries'll be gone soon," I finally told Raven in desperation. "If we don't go now we'll miss them."

"Let's go this evening," he said.

"Let's set a time."

"I'll have the chores done by six. We'll leave then."

"It's dark at eight."

"We'll have to pick fast."

At 6:00 we gathered baskets, drove the few miles to the forest, and hiked riverward, wearing hog boots in hopes that no snake would be able to penetrate them. I had forgotten how far from the road the thicket was—almost a mile, which can be walked in fifteen minutes. In another half mile we'd reach the river.

I was tromping along, enjoying the evening tranquility—all was quiet, the heat abated—and my escape from work. Young longleaf were sending up new bunches of needles, vividly green, chlorophyllic, among soft and springlike wiregrass. White evening glories were blooming, as was a lavender flower I didn't recognize, or perhaps whose name at one time had known but had, with my poor memory, forgotten. Wild indigo was already setting seeds.

I began to smell smoke and then to see clouds of smoky patches through the trees.

"There's been a fire," I said.

"Remember the smoke we saw in the sky? I bet that was a prescribed burn."

"Was that yesterday?"

"Maybe the day before."

We came to the edge of the burn. Two weeks before, when we hiked through, this was a spring-green, growing forest. Now, everything was scorched. The ground was black, trunks of pines charred, logs still smoking. In a few spots across the vast woods I could see flames, old heart pine stumps still afire. A pine snake had been trapped by the flames and lay dead beside the path. The ground smoked in places, and I worried about my gum boots melting.

Woodpeckers had knocked rotten bark off and drilled holes into the timber of one snag, and now fire was consuming the dead tree. It leaned, weakening. Below that tree—in its path, should it have fallen—lay the thicket of blackberries we had scouted out a fortnight earlier and about which we had been dreaming, their color changed from midnight black to a weak purple.

"We missed them," I said.

"May be."

"They're burned."

It was true. The berries had been toasted. I tasted one. It was awful.

"Shoot," I said. "My mouth's been watering for these for two weeks."

Fire is a natural thing. I couldn't be disappointed. I would not have wanted to be the pine snake, but we know that for the ecosystem of pine flatwoods to continue, for hardwoods not to overtake the pines, it has to burn. The system evolved with fire, with lightning, and with fire it continues. Fire brings life.

To understand fire in these terms is not easy, but the Indians saw fire this way: fire was natural, fire was a tool, fire was housecleaning. The first settlers saw it like this, and the folks who still burn their woods see it.

Fire is the element that connects the river to its uplands. Fire runs through the pine flatwoods and is stopped in its tracks by wetness. Fire is what keeps the wetlands in the wetlands. Otherwise, floodplain trees creep upslope and change the nature of the flatwoods.

We poked around the thicket, one eye on the burning, leaning snag.

"I see some green in there," Raven said.

He and I pushed inward through the stickers, toward brambles that still carried green leaves. In the center of the thicket, where the canes were sturdy and more than head-tall, the fire had not penetrated, and here the blackberries were succulent, black, an inch and a half long, hanging in gorgeous clumps. A cool, rainy spring had been good to the plants; they were redolent with fruit.

We ate our fill and picked enough for a pie, a smoky blackberry river pie.

I read somewhere once that every cell of the body is replaced in seven years. In order to become of a place, cell by cell, one needs to consume what it produces. That's why I eat blackberry pie, river-made; I am renewing the cells of my heart.

CHAPTER 9 *Dreaming Big to Save the Red Bay*

Every time I go to the woods, I expect amazement—crashing black bear, glimpse of a panther—and a kayak trip on Cathead Creek was no exception.

At the canoe outpost in Darien, guide Danny Grisette had papered the walls with topo maps floor to ceiling. When I arrived, he traced where we'd be exploring, through the canals of a historic rice field in McIntosh County, into Buffalo Swamp, drained by Cathead Creek, a tributary of the Altamaha River.

As we paddled through banks of southern wild rice and red-stemmed amaranth drooping with seed, I grooved on how gorgeous fall is in Georgia. The maples are deep as burgundy wine, tupelos flash and fling their red sequins. Sweet gums are pasted with gold stars.

I mean, I was ecstatic. The skies were clear and the air iridescent. The sun was canted and calm. The day was mind-blowingly, awesomely, incredibly beautiful, the way fall is down here in the South.

We saw woodpeckers. We heard deer and wild hogs. Best of all, we got to see a rattlesnake about as long as a hoe handle swimming across the creek. Swimming! Just as happy as you please!

But I saw something else. Among the cypress and maple, tupelo and gum, I saw red bay dying.

Entire trees, large and small, were dead: a die-off in progress.

Red bay is an evergreen with wide, aromatic leaves that is taken for granted in southern forests. You don't pay much attention until you notice how many are dead.

The die-off is caused by a beetle, the red bay ambrosia beetle, first discovered near Savannah in 2002, apparently imported from Asia on wood packaging. The beetle carries a fungus, laurel wilt, which it introduces to a tree and then farms. Actually the fungus, not the beetle, kills the tree.

The beetle is marching through Georgia and beyond, and nothing has been found to stop it. It has spread to South Carolina and Florida, and will not stop there. It will work its way through the red bay's range, the coastal plain of the South.

We can blame the fire ant on Alabama, but this one's on us.

Right now, go out and find a red bay, and hug it, because, unless we find some way to stop the ambrosia beetle, we are watching a die-off of the magnitude of the American chestnut tree decimation.

And don't transport firewood. If a red bay dies in your yard, do not give away the wood. Urge counties susceptible to laurel wilt to enact restrictions on the movement of firewood. Keep the beetle and its fungus confined.

I can't imagine the South without red bays. I can't imagine the Altamaha.

CHAPTER 10   *Center of the Known World*

The Altamaha is irrepressibly and exotically beautiful. Mississippi kites swoop low over the fields and clearings and come to rest in snags on the bars, and the pinckneya looks spangled with lipstick kisses when it blooms. I cannot talk about the beauty, however, without telling you the bad. The very bad. Nuke-plant bad.

There are three things nobody, nobody, wants to live near, and they are mountaintop removal, a coal plant, and a nuclear plant. All three of them will kill you. They may take a while, but they will murder you dead as a doornail. Your sweet life with its milky cups of coffee in the mornings and its perfume of four-o'clocks at nightfall will be cut short long before your time.

In the 1970s, when I was in junior high, government leaders in my home county of Appling engaged in a series of meetings—some public, most not—with the paid chicken hawks of the electric utility industry. Not thinking of Marie Curie, and not knowing yet of Three Mile Island, Chernobyl, or Fukushima, none of these having happened yet, our neighbors, whom my parents helped elect to lead us, voted to allow a nuclear plant to be built on the northern edge of the county, exactly on the banks of the river. In 1975 the twin reactors went online.

I'm sure the people who made this decision were good people. I'm sure they loved their children. I'm sure they thought they were doing the right thing. But they allowed a monster among us. They allowed a secret killer that drags its dirty fogs about our houses at night, leaving even our grass and thus our milk poisoned with radiation.

The same stuff, invisible though it may be, that killed Madame Curie dead as a hammer.

Imagine not being able to see the cancer-causing particles contained in the air you breathe.

༄ I have never made one dime off the nuclear plant. Oh, it has benefitted me. I have availed myself of its power, no doubt, though less through choice than lack of. Plant Hatch supplies 10 percent of Georgia's electricity and sends power to thirty-nine of the forty-two electric membership cooperatives. I am plugged in. And I live nearby. Almost unavoidably, some of the people local to it, the people who reap the grimness and death, reap the energy, too.

This is a source of great personal conflict for me. Being connected to the grid while opposing the grid is like being nice to a person who has robbed you and, if he catches you alone and vulnerable, will rob you again. I want more than anything to kick in the teeth of this monster. This means if I had the money, I would call the solar power people in Savannah *today* to come put panels on my roof.

I'll tell you what else it means. It means I cut off my water heater until I need it. Ten minutes before I need to wash dishes, I flip the breaker on. The air conditioner stays off. I unplug everything, always. If I have the choice of making butter by shaking the jar or using the blender, I shake the jar.

Should I go on? The appliances are energy-efficient. I hang my laundry on a line. I don't own a blow-dryer. I don't own a toaster. I don't own a microwave. I don't own an electric Crock-Pot or shaver or hundreds of other ridiculous nonessentials that, were they sitting in my house, would fill me daily with anger and despair, knowing as I know the connection between them and the loss of what I love. That nuclear plant is humming away, filling the river with hot water and the skies with radiated steam, because people want massage chairs and whirlpool tubs and enough Christmas lights to emblazon the Taj Mahal.

No, thank you.

Until I am old and worn out and my bones are brittle as toothpicks, I will choose to do things by hand rather than give any extra credence to the energy running from that plant into every wall of my home. But by then I'll be disconnected from it. I'll be connected to the sun, lovely old Mr. Sun riding high up in the sky, looking down at us in disbelief. "You've got a perfectly great nuke plant up here," he's saying. "The energy is free. I'm sending it down most every day, enough for everybody, yours for the taking."

Come on, people.

Turn off the switch.

Shut down the plant.

෴ I live within the ten-mile radius of Plant Hatch, as I have for most of my life. When I lived with Silas at my grandparents' farm in Appling County, I would come home on Wednesdays to the weather radio blaring in the house. It was the weekly test. Sometimes, if I arrived after dark, the noise scared me. I thought people were inside my house, talking.

If bad weather was forecast, the alert radio let us know. If there was a thunderstorm two counties over, it let us know. It never let us know that tritium was leaking. It never let us know just how close the plant got one flawed day to a meltdown. It didn't let us know when another culvert had been plugged with spent nuclear rods. Because company officials don't want to ruin their reputation by divulging the truth.

Only days after I moved to the Tattnall County farm where I now live, plant safety personnel showed up at my house with a new weather alert radio. This one still clicks on once a week, Wednesdays, as a test. But somebody got smart and designed it so that after a few minutes, if nobody shuts it off, the radio deactivates on its own.

The older radios were triggered constantly by weather and by the Wednesday tests, and people got tired of the intrusion. People didn't trust that the radio would help them in an emergency anyway. They unplugged them. They tossed them in back rooms. They gave them away. At least my neighbors in the ten-mile nuclear fallout radius now are more apt to leave their radios plugged in. In a nuclear emergency, now they have a fighting chance.

My local leaders sold us down the river. Georgia Power took the land, they took lives, I believe, they left their pollution, they despoiled our skies and river. What I got was a weather radio.

Twice I have toured the nuclear plant. The first time, I was a kid, and my class took a field trip to the visitors' center. Believe me, the industry didn't want to build the visitors' center. It's a waste of money. It has to be air-conditioned and staffed by a pretty woman who knows nothing about meltdowns. All industry wanted to build was the basics. But they had to add a visitors' center. Otherwise, their presence would say this: *Too dangerous to visit. Do not pause along the roadway to gaze or gawk. We're taking what we can from you illiterate rednecks and leaving you the mess. You're too dumb to understand nuclear physics anyway.*

My classmates and I saw the cold, sterile displays explaining nuclear fission, the maps of cooling towers and containment pools. (Are you noticing the language?) The sleek visitors' center made the nuclear plant look acceptable, profitable, inviting. It made it seem like an asset to the region. The pretty receptionist gave us a lollipop. Oh, what a nice gift for the little pinkneck savages. Let them get tooth decay before they get cancer.

The second trip, I was an adult. My son attended Altamaha Elementary, located about six miles south of the plant. Spent fuel rods had become too numerous for the plant to store any longer, and management was desperate for a place to park them. I mean, the plant had to go to the bathroom bad. It had its legs crossed.

It was looking to Yucca Mountain for storage. As soon as the underground storage was built there, ground zero for the apocalypse, on ancient indigenous sacred grounds—*we have to go to the Indians to find people dumber than these hayseeds*—they could ship out the spent fuel and keep on producing power, regardless of the by-products: Uranium. Plutonium. Cesium-137. Strontium-90.

Radioactive waste decays, yes. But you should be aware that the half-life of cesium-137 and strontium-90 is 30 years. The half-life of plutonium-239 is *24,000 years.* How—tell me this—are we going to label the stuff sitting at Plant Hatch in an open-air nuclear waste dump so that people 24,000 years from now, who may look back on us as being natives, will understand that to approach it is deadly?

A dose of radiation fatal to a human is five hundred rems. Ten years after removal from a nuclear reactor, spent nuclear fuel rods are still emitting into the surrounding environment ten thousand rems per hour.

If radiation gets into the groundwater, then it can enter the food chain.

Yucca Mountain said no. The Nevada governor said no. The Paiute and Shoshone Indians, through whose land the waste would have to travel to reach Yucca Mountain, said no.

What to do, the white collars asked themselves. *Why, I guess we'll have to store the nuclear waste right here. We've got plenty of concrete, heh heh. We'll build us some big culverts and set them on end and put a chainlink fence around them. And we'll blame the government for not finding us a place to put the waste like they promised.*

Yes, we are a private corporation. No, we don't think it's socialism to ask the government to figure out what we're supposed to do with waste.

Oh, the elementary school? Why, that's six miles away. And kids are made of rubber, everybody knows that. They get more radiation every day from cartoons. Or the sun.

It's pretty easy to tell I'm angry. Very angry. The kids who attend this elementary school are human beings. They have little kidneys and little lungs. They have little brains, trying to get big. They have little bones that want to become big strong bones, so they can plant trees that they will later sit under and so they can spin their big brawny and buxom lovers across dance floors.

That's what's at stake.

I toured the storage site so that public relations shills for the plant could show me how safe these turned-up culverts are, with a chainlink fence and everything. And see here, we have a Geiger counter wired to the fence and as you can see, the radiation, even this close, is barely registering.

Like the tritium leaks are not registering.

Like the overheated water is not registering.

Like the radiation is released in the steam in amounts too small to register.

Like the radiation in cow's milk wasn't registering—well, maybe it was registering, but we only had to test for a year, and we aren't required to do that anymore.

∽ It's time to talk about the hardest thing of all. The deaths. Leukemia. Brain cancer. Lung cancer, but the person smoked. Lupus. More leukemia. Pancreatic cancer. Lung cancer and the person never smoked. Cancer all over. Six-year-old cancer. Baby cancer. Old cancer. Cancer up and down the river corridor. Stomach cancer. Esophageal cancer. Ovarian cancer. There's a cancer for every part of the body, because the pollutants go everywhere. The pollutants that cause cells to mutate go everywhere.

The person with the lung cancer who never smoked was my mother. She had breast cancer at the same time. All her life she lived within ten miles of the plant. Explain that, Dr. Doolittle.

I'm being unfair, you're saying. Rates of cancer are high everywhere. Yes, they are. But you explain this—explain that the plant is *not* a contributing factor. Do the epidemiological studies you know you need to do and give us proof that your cancer-causing plant is not causing our cancer.

If it's not your fault, then we'll look elsewhere. To our chemical pesticides and fertilizers. To processed food. To preservatives in food. To chemicals in our homes.

Because until you're exonerated, Plant Hatch, in my mind, you're guilty.

Question to readers: Who have you known who has worked at a nuclear plant, been exposed to radiation, and died of cancer? Send me the answer. We'll start there. We'll start our own study.

Once my uncle told me a story about catching a flathead that had swallowed a small catfish. The catfish ruptured the flathead's floater, so the flathead wouldn't stay down. It was floating near the surface, and my uncle's friend caught it easily. "We didn't know what was wrong with it," my uncle said. "We were afraid it might be getting something from the nuclear plant."

That uncle is dead, of cancer.

❧   When I trained to be a hospice volunteer, my class did a death awareness exercise. On little squares of paper we named ten things we really love, and, one by one, we crumpled them up and threw them away. My farm—to the trash. My husband—to the trash. To have to give up flowers, or books, or my son—although I know I will say goodbye one day to everything precious—almost breaks my heart in two.

It was just a thought exercise.

But it's happening every day. We are destroying the things we love.

❧   With climate disruption, of course, that's what we humans are doing. We are throwing away the things most beautiful and meaningful to us, things we've thought immutable: predictable seasons, weather we can trust, polar bears, coastlines, entire islands, permafrost, glaciers.

Imagine throwing away glaciers.

With climate disruption, we throw away the cool holes in the river where the sturgeon find refuge. We throw away ancient patterns of rainfall and flow. What else we will be forced to toss is anybody's guess.

In the summer of 2007, a heat wave lingered over the South for eleven straight days, killing more than fifty people and setting all kinds of weather records. Somewhere, almost every day, an old record was trumped—hundreds of new record highs. Nashville, Tennessee, registered fifteen days above 100 degrees in August, the most recorded for any month; on August 22 the thermometer peaked at 102 blistering degrees, a new daily record. The hot South had never been hotter.

Alabama's Browns Ferry nuclear plant shut down one of its reactors when the Tennessee River became too hot for cooling the plant, the first time such a thing had happened in the United States.

In the middle of all this global-warming "paranoia," we hear nuclear energy touted as a "green" energy. How green is an energy that produces as its number-one by-product a substance that will instantly kill any man, woman, or beast who comes in contact with it, and will fundamentally alter anything that gets within its reach, and that will not go away for tens, maybe hundreds, of thousands of years? How long before the culverts break down? Which, by the way, erode as easily and as quickly as any concrete bridge (and you can look underneath one to see that).

None of us wants to lose that which we love. Changing light bulbs isn't enough. Paddling rivers is nothing. We need life-saving legislation, and Congress is not going to act unless we pressure them to do so.

Here's what I think the United States should do about climate disruption: Reduce greenhouse gas emissions by 80 percent by the year 2050. Reduce permissible carbon dioxide levels to 350 parts per million, at most. Use that target to set an annual carbon cap. Set a personal carbon ration, a free annual quota for every person, to be spent on gas and electricity, train and plane tickets.

Meanwhile, invest in our rail system. Set emission limits on vehicles made and sold in the country. Abandon all road-building and road-widening projects and freeze airport construction. Ban the construction of new coal-fired power plants.

Set building regulations that impose requirements for energy efficiency. Set minimum efficiency standards for appliances. Ban the sale of wasteful technologies such as patio heaters and garden floodlights. Redeploy money earmarked for new nuclear missiles toward alternative energy research.

If you still have the muscle tone and the energy to paddle a boat, get rid of your motor. Get yourself a little dugout or a kayak or a rowboat. Get yourself some peace and quiet. Get yourself some health, some skinniness.

◠ Around 2000 the Edwin I. Hatch Nuclear Plant, owned by Southern Company, petitioned the Nuclear Regulatory Commission to renew its permit to operate for another twenty-five years. The NRC appeared unconcerned that the plant was planned to last only twenty-five years. It appeared unconcerned about high cancer rates in the corridor. It appeared unconcerned about thermal pollution in the river, about the fact that where the heated plume enters the river the temperature is several degrees hotter than it is at its hottest naturally, and with global warming getting hotter, this could wipe out some of the more thermally dependent species.

I've had my say. I took my stand at the public hearings and in letters to the NRC, and I take my stand here. I stand with the sturgeon and the redbreast, with the children and the nursing mothers. I stand with innocent passersby and grieving widows. I stand with the activist who presented a Toilet Seat Award to the NRC. I stand with the Paiute and the Shoshone.

CHAPTER 11 *Night Fishing with the Senator*

Any place can be deep and far away, but few are deeper and farther than the wild country of the lower Altamaha. Everything here was created on a grand scale.

At its mouth, the Altamaha's flood plain is five miles wide. It cleaves into four distributaries—called rivers too, each voluminous, startling in capacity—that empty from the continent one-third of Georgia's water. The four channels (Darien, Butler, Champney, and Altamaha) wash through salt marsh and old cypress, unbraiding into creeks that swell with eight-foot tides and when they drain become long limbs of black mud. The mud seems alive. It bubbles and brews.

Here land and water are in constant discourse. Here eagles construct their haphazard aeries.

There is a fish to match the spirit of a water body. To rival the Altamaha delta a fish must be tigerish and fierce and untended. Big things live in big water.

Here are the catfish.

And not just any old catfish.

I am night fishing with my state senator, who is Republican. I am Democrat if anything, or maybe Progressive Socialist Green. My history with my senator has not been placid. We have been friends a long time now, but that doesn't stop us from arguing. We have more than once entered the arena of political debate with crests cocked and spurs distended, and have flown at each other. This law or that. This amendment or that. This right or that.

My senator argues that poor people who can't afford more than a quarter-acre of land should be able to install a septic system. I believe he's using a democratic argument to further a right-wing cause, which is more development. I argue pollution and quality of life: Why would people want to live so close? Why should the earth bear this burden?

He wants to know what harm would be done to mine the downed cypress and longleaf, lost during the rafting days and preserved underwater in the Altamaha. I say, why do we have to take everything? Why can't some things be left alone? Why can't the fish keep those logs? Wouldn't to take them be stealing?

Despite our disagreements, we are bound in a tentative alliance, a wavering but undeniable friendship. In some ways we're like siblings. Blond and boyish, Tommie Williams is a good politician, and even if he doesn't vote my way, he listens.

Tonight, Dorset Hurley is our guide. He's a strong, lean biologist whose angular face is softened and made mobile by kindness, at the eyes and mouth, and by a freshly graying beard. He reminds me of apples, because he looks so healthy and because of his name—Dorset Golden is one of the two key apple varieties that produce in subtropical southern Georgia.

The senator has won this fishing trip at a fundraiser and has invited me along.

When Dorset meets us at Champney, a landing near Darien, at 5:00 p.m., he doesn't say much, but you can tell a lot about a person from his or her boat, and his Carolina Skiff is whitewashed and spotless, organized, nothing out of place. I don't trust just any guide in the wild, but I know immediately that Dorset won't get into any trouble he can't get out of. And for some reason I think that if I get in a boat that's scrubbed clean, there's a good chance I'll come back alive.

As we motor upriver, Dorset names landmarks, the wind snatching words from his mouth and throwing pieces of them back at us: Champney River, Two Way Fish Camp, South River, Butler Island. He is taking us to his sacred hole. We'll try for some of the big flatheads, he says, but for sure we'll catch channels.

State land, wildlife management area, Dorset points out. Lot of turkey. The senator is behind me and can't hear what Dorset is saying. I turn around and repeat everything verbatim to the senator.

I remember once sitting in the senator's office in Atlanta, door closed, hollering at him about the importance of setbacks on trout streams (a law that did not pass). I'm the environmentalist, but the senator loves to fish, and so there's hope. On the way here we argued again, this time about the Roadless Initiative, an act signed into law by President Clinton during his last days in office that protects the remaining unroaded areas in our national forests from logging. The senator and I were not arguing about roadless areas, or the need for them, really, but about the Forest Service's ability to pass such a resolution. The senator believes a lead governing body should make decisions. Often our discussions come down to the Constitution, to who's supposed to make laws—as a lawmaker the senator wants to retain these abilities, the control.

Sometimes I think his eclectic arguments are smokescreens, ways to avoid the real issues, ways to cloud ideology with tactics, something the Georgia Republicans are very good at.

"Did you approve as law the four-laning of this road?" I asked as we drove coastward, vexed, motioning out the Isuzu's window at Highway 341. "No. Agencies make decisions. That's why we *have* agencies. Besides, if something is good, why does it matter from what corner it comes?"

"Our system of checks and balances was set up to prevent despotism," Tommie rejoined. "Otherwise we'd have anarchy."

"What's so wrong with anarchy? What we have now is democracy by purchase. The most money wins."

Politics are transitory intrigue, yes, but the political system dictates our lives, mine and his: mine because I care about what happens to nature and wildness (and I see that most of our laws are destroying the environment), and the senator's because he cares about capitalism.

When we get to Dorset's honey hole, a bend in the South channel, which is the main flow of the Altamaha, the men sink an anchor at each end of the boat. Two ropes hurry from their quoyles for long minutes until finally they idle, and the men tie off the ropes at the cleats. The water is sixty-five feet deep here. The tide is coming in and the moon is new, the best time to fish. Dorset sets us up with rods and reels, which we bait with fat frozen shrimp. I confess that this is one of the few times that I have fished with serious intent. For me, going fishing means reading a book while a friend fishes, although one year in a saltwater creek near Tybee Island, trying for sea bass, I reeled in a stingray, a terrible haul that required two people to unhook.

"Basically," Dorset says, "drop the bait overboard and click when it hits bottom, a long way down. It takes fifteen minutes for them to smell the bait." Around us the river is olive-gray, turgid, and we are diminished to a white toy boat, three cornhusk dolls dangling our invisible lines. There is so much water, infinitely greater than us, a magnitude not to reckon with.

"Yep," Dorset says. "Big floodplain rivers demand respect. Dams give, roads buckle, houses float."

For some reason he gives me the heaviest rod. "If you get the big fish," he says, "you'll be glad you have it." The reel is an old Penn, the kind for which you have to use your finger to stop it from peeing all over itself. Two or three times the line ends up in a bird's nest, but Dorset is nice about it. The thirty-pound test sings and sings as it unwinds, down and down. It lands uneventfully on the bottom.

We wait twenty, twenty-five, thirty minutes. There is nothing, not even a tug. The only problem with this place is the interstate is a quarter mile away, a double-bridge monolith erected above the salt marsh and tidal floodplain. Tractor trailers loaded with new cars roar toward Florida.

"I don't understand why they're not biting," Dorset says. "The conditions are perfect." We recast with the tide. I feel a tug on my line and turn to find the senator pulling at my monofilament, grinning.

"Hey!" I say. I turn to Dorset.

"Reckon our talking is hurting our fishing?"

Both men grin. I have set myself up for two of the great jesters of the South.

"We've been wondering when you'd hush," Tommie says. "That's what we get for bringing a woman."

"We didn't want to hurt your feelings, so we didn't say anything," Dorset joins in.

But he can't hold a joke long. "Talk all you want," he says. "The fish sixty-five feet down can't hear what you say."

At that moment, a few hundred feet away from the skiff, a fish leaps sideways. It is at least four feet long and wiggles midair before it crashes back into the molten water.

"Sturgeon," I yelp and point.

It is a shortnose sturgeon, which, despite my loquaciousness, I am the only one who sees.

At one time the sturgeon migrated upriver in scores to spawn. Now they are endangered.

Now that I have seen one, let's talk about sturgeon. Two species live in the Altamaha, Atlantic and shortnose. They are among the largest freshwater fish in the world, each weighing as much as one thousand pounds. They grow old, up to sixty years. They are found also in the Ogeechee and Savannah rivers in Georgia, south to the St. Johns in Florida, and north to Canada. They are believed to spawn near bluffs.

"Sturgeon require relatively cool, fresh water with a good supply of oxygen," says ichthyologist Doug Shaw. "So areas of hot water or low oxygen act as barriers to sturgeon movement just as effectively as dams."

In summer the half- to two-degree Celsius change in water temperature is enough to bother them. Summers, they flee to the lower areas of the Altamaha, where freshwater springs are likely to flow.

The fish can tolerate some salinity, twenty-one parts per million for the Atlantic and nineteen for the shortnose, to be exact. They hunker near springs, artesian seeps, or deeper holes. They don't move around much. They lose weight.

Groundwater withdrawal, then, is hazardous to sturgeon, depending on the effect the withdrawal has on spring flows. Thermal pollution, such as that from mills and plants on the river, also has a negative effect on the long-term health of the sturgeon population.

This brings me again to climate change. By now we understand that burning coal, gas, and oil releases carbon dioxide, and that CO_2 and other gases have become trapped in the atmosphere and have begun to heat the planet. Dramatically. The temperature is rising. We're setting record hot temperatures every summer.

Nine of the ten warmest years on record have occurred since 1990. No longer is there any doubt about the reason: global climate disruption, caused by fossil fuel emissions and by deforestation. Temperature rise is transforming our physical geography and climate, as well as the way we live.

If climate change heats up the river water, the sturgeon are going to suffer. They may have to leave, fin north. (For the same reason, south Georgia is home to more and more Florida birds, such as the roseate spoonbill.) As weather patterns alter the populations of forage fish, the sturgeon may get hungry. They may not be able to evolve as quickly as conditions demand.

One night, Dorset recounts, about 2:00 in the morning, a shortnose sturgeon leaped from the water and landed in his boat. This very boat. He is still awestruck, telling it. "It must've been seven feet long. A hundred pounds. You can wait in a boat your whole life and not have that happen," he says.

Why would a fish do such a thing? Why would a fish that is so big suddenly fling itself out of a perfectly good river into a foreign environment, the air, twist sideways, and belly-flop back in? Perhaps to rid itself of a bothersome barnacle or fish, much like a dog will outrun a horsefly? Perhaps for delight?

Our lines are limp, hanging. Nothing. After another half hour Dorset says, "Let's try someplace else."

When next we stop, we are far up Lewis Creek, a primary and wild run of the river. The creek cradles Lewis Island, holy land, home to the ancient cypress.

Tonight on the river, white ibis recompose the evening trees. Rafts of purple false dragonheads sail on the small islands, blooming at the edge of the cut-grass stands. Here an osprey. Here a tree swallow snatching a delicate ivory caddis fly from the air.

At Poppell's Bluff, we fish toward the red-sand face of the bluff, near snags where we hope the channel cats will be hiding. The sand is like a tablet on which the history of the place is written. Bleached oyster shells tumble toward two holes in the bank that nobody knows what animal might occupy.

Another thirty minutes. Nothing. Two kayakers slip upriver.

"Seen a good campsite?" one of them asks.

"We came from the other way," Dorset says. "Maybe a little farther down on the right?"

Dusk is sneaking fast upon the land, and with it an armada of thunderous clouds, all the time thicker and meaner, like a basket of dark plums tumbling toward us, snuffing out the sunset, until we're manning the sky as much as we are our lines. It's going to storm, soon. The question is whether it will storm where we are.

Wood storks and egrets and herons fly roostward. Around us the water, at high tide, fidgets. The wind finds us and begins nudging. Rain's close.

"Stay or go?" Dorset asks, wonderfully democratic. Downriver there is an opening in the sky of lambent and muted yellow, through which we might slip and avoid a drenching.

"Let's go," says the senator. He has brought a rain jacket and puts it on.

I didn't bring one. "I don't mind getting wet," I say. I strip down to my bathing suit and stash my clothes in a drywell.

Leaving is like ducking out of a bar fight, feeling bold to be escaping so easily and unscathed. The rain comes anyway, hurling cold little pits at us as we bolt downriver. The senator peers through his hood, watching an osprey that has tagged us since Lewis Island, which occasionally shakes her body midflight as if to dispense a burden of rain. I huddle behind Dorset, warmed by my life vest.

To the west, at our backs, a violet curtain surrounds us like a theater, us on stage in our clean little boat. Then the lightning lopes north, and we escape the worst of the storm, until the sky only drizzles. Back at the honey hole we stop. Now water is coming at us from three directions: Pouring tannic-stained and siltified out of Georgia. Pulled brackish by the moon from the ocean. Dropping fresh, maybe acidic, from the sky.

The evening flees. Over on the interstate, passing cars light small sections of darkness. We are still small, after all. Suddenly the senator gets a bite, the first, sets the hook with a jerk and reels in a gaff-topsail, a saltwater catfish with stiff barbels. Immediately, before we get a look at it, Dorset scoops it up and heaves it overboard.

"That's a bad boy," he says. "It'll tear you up." Whatever that means.

The Senator gets another bite. This is obviously a big one. We hurriedly reel in all the other lines and watch the senator, reeling with his left hand, arching and spinning, reeling. This goes on for a long time. He is working hard, and I can see when he starts to tire. He's breathing hard. He's out of shape, I am thinking, chuckling to myself. Too much sitting in the Senate chambers. Dorset has hung a lantern from a bent rebar pole, and in the dim light we see a huge fish as it surfaces. Dorset readies a net.

Dorset gets excited when the channel catfish is finally in the boat, and when he gets excited, he starts to curse. "That's a damn nice fish," he says. He's gleeful, jiggling the skiff. "Look at that son of a bitch. Godamighty, what a fish." He uses stronger language too. The senator says nothing.

The fish is trophy-size, almost three feet long. Maybe fifteen years old, Dorset says, and so perfect, so damn gorgeous, it could be used as a type specimen.

"You can tell people you caught one this big," Dorset says, pausing to hold his thumb and forefinger about five inches apart, "between the eyes."

"Even if it's an old fish it doesn't get big unless it has a highly productive food source, all the way down the food chain." Dorset turns scientific. "This fish is indicative of the health of the river, which is a direct indicator of the quality of life for human habitation." That's why the river system is home to 125 species of flora and fauna. Is the senator listening?

Dorset is saying how lucky we are.

The senator is especially lucky. I suspect he has always been so. Luck comes to the brave, my friend says, but we all have lines out, all baited the same, with an identical fat crescent of shrimp at the end. Tommie gets the third strike, too, and pulls in *another* channel cat, this one twenty inches.

"Maybe I'll take a break," Tommie says now. "I'm tired from all this fishing."

He is making me mad.

All of us are watching the tips of our rods. I am holding mine and there is nothing. I am hoping somewhere sixty-five feet below, an ancient catfish is moving in.

After Tommie's flurry of luck, we are quiet. The only sounds are the lost melodies of red-winged blackbirds in spartina. The drizzle has stopped altogether, and occasionally there is a fleeing splash or gurgle of river. I want to remind the senator that we have not seen a house all night—the floodplain is its own setback—and the wildness is primal and absolute.

Tommie lets me cast out the back of the boat, where he has been. He punches me, and in the light of the lantern he makes the gesture of tucking the thumb under the armpit, fist closed, gloating.

I shake my head and start to say something, but he makes the sign to hush, finger across his lips, and points at the water. He and I both have a huge competitive streak.

Right away I feel a nibble at the tip of the rod. Dorset says the channels will grab the shrimp—attack!—and that I should keep hold of the rod. Don't let go. Once he was fishing with a buddy who didn't have a grip on the rod. When the guy got a bite, the fish pulled the rod, a good one that Dorset hated losing, right out of his hands.

"But we got it back," Dorset laughs. "We caught him again, later that night. He was still attached to the other rod!"

For a second, feeling the fish, I play with the line and without even realizing what I am doing I stand up and set the hook.

The men are reeling in the other lines. The fish swims through one, starts to tangle, and Dorset speedily clips the line. This is another big one, they think.

I really don't know how to catch a fish, I'm ashamed to say. I'd like to be better at it. The senator coaches me. "Arch the rod. Now reel. Arch, reel," he says. "That's it."

"Thanks," I say to him. "I need the help."

"You're doing fine," he says.

The fish is big and doesn't want to come to the surface. But I am bigger and my will is greater, plus my mind has been studying catching him, an advantage he doesn't have. He has been tracing the bottom of the river, memorizing the pattern of snags and the habits of darters. Maybe he has been guarding eggs and is hungry, studying the nicety of shrimp. He has not been thinking of how to escape me.

"This is a lot of reeling," I say.

"He took a lot of line," Dorset replies, with a word of encouragement. *Arch and reel. Pull.* "Don't be afraid to bend the rod or put pressure on the line. Neither will break."

Landing the fish seems to take forever, me holding the rod arched toward the boat, the fish still unseen. Fighting me. Fighting the line, which is all I have to hold him. The fish is exhausting me. I am making small noises as I work the rod, struggling, wheezes that come from deep inside, and also I begin apologizing: To the senator, for teasing him. To Hemingway. To all fisherpeople. Finally I understand *The Old Man and the Sea* as something more than literature.

Dip, reel more line, pull. The fish is fighting me hard. He does not want his fine life interrupted. He is a fish of power. He has survived thus far because of his power. My right hand aches.

"This is like having a baby," I gasp. Or like wrestling a calf. Or an alligator, which I have not actually done. The fish-catching is short, maybe five minutes in all, but five hard and time-stopping minutes. Slowly, slowly the giant fish rises through sixty-five feet of water, through layers of darkness and fluctuations of pressure, from the coolness of seepage springs toward the warmth of southern summers. I feel him—or her—ten or fifteen feet below the boat, and I am battling now, the rod tucked beneath my arm, pulling with my body.

"The reason they fight so hard," Dorset told me later, "is tidal influence. They have to fight their whole lives to adjust to it." They have to lead normal lives with one hundred thousand gallons of fresh water a minute rolling downstream at them. The big river made the fish powerful.

I, then, pull against all the force of the outgoing tide, and of the gravity of the emptying river, and also the cloud-thick sky. And I bring back the entire sea in a fish, and the universe, and when the senator scoops it out of the night waters, it is a channel catfish possibly a hair bigger than his own, the first one. I never dreamed I could catch such a thing.

I talk to the fish, which is gasping in the floor of the boat, thanking it for its long life and for the secrets it brings to me. Dorset and Tommie may think I'm weird, but I don't care. I am so grateful. When I eat the fish, I will eat the river I love. I have been inducted into a mythology.

The time is late, close to midnight, and we don't want to fish any more. Our exhaustion is more than physical; there is something else a fish takes out of you, something you have to give up to land one. I don't know what it is, but something is spent. Taking an animal that has lived in a place as wildly grand as the Altamaha delta for fifteen years is an act of magnitude.

Afterward, there is exhilaration, there is food for the tribe, but there is also a hollow spot in the spirit.

We tidy up and head back to the landing in darkness, trusting Dorset's navigation. Wet, our hair clumped to our heads, the senator and I take pictures under the streetlamps, flashes in the night. The three fish are heavy, full of an underwater life we will never know. Later, when we weigh them, the biggest two are fifteen and sixteen pounds, thirty-one and thirty-two inches in length. We don't know who caught the larger one, but I believe that I did.

All the long drive inland, the senator and I do not argue.

Catfish Stew

2–3 quarts water
4 pounds catfish
1 stick butter
1 medium onion, chopped
Salt and pepper, to taste
⅓ cup plain corn meal
⅓ cup self-rising flour
1 egg
½ cup cream
1 cup fresh milk
Hot sauce

Place water, catfish, butter, onions, salt and pepper in a large stockpot. Cook until fish is tender. Cool and remove bones from catfish. Break up meat and put back in pot. Mix meal, flour, egg, and both types of milk until smooth; add to catfish mixture. Continue to stir with whisk on medium heat until mixture thickens. If too thick, add more milk. Add hot sauce if desired.

CHAPTER 12   *Black Bear*

When I wander through the Altamaha swamps, something is missing and I want it back. It was here before. It was here before my people ever got here. It was even here before the Creeks arrived. It was an original inhabitant, but we killed it off, every one, and now none are left. I want it back.

Okefenokee Swamp has them. The north Georgia mountains still have them. The Chattahoochee National Forest still has them. The Great Smoky Mountains have them. Even central Florida still has them.

In some of those places they are so numerous that they are still hunted. In Okefenokee people hunt them with dogs.

But none in the Altamaha. None in a place where they could again find a luxuriant, welcoming home.

"The habitat is there," a biologist friend told me, "to support black bears. The bears are not restricted to floodplains and wetlands. They use a wide variety of habitats. They'll even use managed forests, including clear-cuts with blackberry thickets. When I say the habitat is there in the Altamaha corridor, I'm talking uplands too."

"What are we waiting on?" I asked.

"Bears come with some nuisance complaints," my friend said. "They get into bird feeders and garbage cans. We need a population that is willing to accept them. So far there hasn't been the government support needed to bring them back."

Let me ask you this. If you lived in a place and someone came and took you away, and carried you to live in Timbuktu, wouldn't you most likely be wanting to get back home? Maybe you fell in love with a Timbuktuvian and married. Maybe you had children and began to feel quite at home. But in the middle of the night, something would call to you and you would wake from a sad dream, yearning, with tears running down your face. Deep in your bones, you would pine for your homeland. It made you. It doesn't go away.

The place would miss you too. Think of your favorite place in nature, some warm, grassy spot where you can lie listening to the river murmuring as it runs, with the sun filtering through a river birch onto your face. You fall asleep and the birch moves its leaves to block the sun from your eyes. When you get up and leave—go back to your job, back to your happy home—something sinks behind you. Do you think that place doesn't miss you?

Do you think the Altamaha doesn't weep for its lost bears?

Our motherland weeps for her lost children.

"I think that eventually," my friend said to me, "bears may get back to the Altamaha basin on their own. The state's northern population is expanding."

"Okefenokee is less than one hundred miles away."

"Yes. Okefenokee is closer," he said.

"How many years will a resettlement take?" I asked.

"Bears don't expand rapidly," he said. "The problem is that females tend to establish a home range near their natal range. Males are the ones who typically make excursions. So the movement as a population is at a snail's pace."

"Are you saying that what we need is a sow to move in? Because the chance of a male arriving is good?"

"More or less," he said. "We need both, but there's a better chance of a male arriving than a female. The question is, would it make sense and would people support speeding up the process?"

"Has it been done successfully elsewhere?"

"Oh, yes," he said. "Louisiana and Mississippi have reintroduced black bears successfully. What we've found is that we need to move a sow with very young cubs. The cubs help keep her at the new site over the winter. But it's a lot of work. Biologists have to find a sow with the right-aged cubs."

"What is the public opinion?"

"We have pretty good support for reintroduction. Especially among hunters. Black bear is a great game animal. If they settled in well in the Altamaha corridor they could eventually be hunted."

Whatever it takes, buddy.

In 2008 University of Georgia professor Craig Miller and graduate student Joshua Agee surveyed residents of middle Georgia about reintroduction of black bears. Four thousand surveys were sent to residents of four counties. From the 1,227 responses, Miller and Agee determined that 61 percent of middle Georgians support the release of black bears. Twenty-one percent had seen a black bear. In general, when people had seen a bear, they more strongly supported reintroduction. Sixty percent were not concerned about possible property damage, and 82 percent said that they considered a wildlife sighting a "positive experience."

We want them back.

What I am hoping for is an adventurous pregnant sow to get fed up with all the herbiciding that the timber companies are doing around Okefenokee Swamp, destroying understory in apocalyptic fashion, and head north for a better life for her kids. She can veer around Waycross, traveling by night, crossing farmland and roads, sticking to the brush, through Ware and Pierce and Appling counties, and that's all it will take. At the north edge of Appling County she will hit the Altamaha. She can settle in at Moody Forest, or Big Hammock, or Bullards Creek.

Come on, girls. Put on your traveling shoes.

Vacancy: We've put out the welcome sign. We've tied a yellow ribbon around the old oak tree. Welcome home.

CHAPTER 13 *Tributary*

We come to a river with a burden in our heart, and for a time the burden is lifted.

It is Independence Day and I come to the river thinking of my husband, whom I have delivered to the Savannah airport with a sheaf of funeral programs in his luggage. I come thinking of his sister, Margaret, three days gone.

I come to the river with bloodstain on my car. It happened when I was returning from the airport, where I dropped Raven for the flight to Rochester and his sister's memorial mass. I was in a hurry to get home, although, in my defense, I was not speeding. I had turned south on State Route 178 in Tattnall County and was traveling through prison land, the ten thousand acres of field and range that have been worked by prisoners for years. Because this land is set aside as agrarian, it is more replete with wildlife than most other places. Often I see wonderful birds.

I had not reached the potter's field, the hillside of unadorned crosses where poor prisoners whose families do not want the bodies, or inmates who no longer have families, are buried. (There are more of them than you think.) From that point thousands of acres of prison farm open up into a gorgeous vista. One could be in Montana.

I was motoring up the small hill there when the second tragedy, the one following Margaret's death, happened. Three birds in some kind of love triangle, some hot-blooded romance, flew out into the road only feet in front of me. There was no time to swerve, no time to brake. *If the birds stay low*, I thought in that instant, *I'll straddle them.* But an overtaken bird does not lay low. It flies toward freedom.

All I could do was plunge over them, too soon done. At my speed there was not much time even to listen for a thump.

The birds were blue grosbeaks, two brilliant males and a brownish female.

I stopped, turned the car around, and parked on the shoulder. A male waited in the middle of the lane, alive, upright, stunned, his wing canted at an odd angle. He was blue as a guard uniform, with rust-orange spots on his wings. He was hurt, perhaps irreparably so, but I could not allow him to die by an oncoming set of vehicle tires.

On the road-edge I noticed the female grosbeak, dead.

I hoped the third bird, nowhere to be seen, was alive somewhere, maybe flown over the hog-wire fence and out into the morning sun, which was coming up over the pines and already touching the graves closest to the road.

I gathered the blue grosbeak quickly in a stained bandanna, careful with its wing, hurriedly retrieved the dead body of the female, and fled the road. A woman near Crawfordville, Florida, once stopped to help a road-wounded heron, which is a large, strong bird. The heron had life enough to fight but not to fly or run. In the woman's drive to rescue the hurt bird, she forgot caution and was killed by a speeding vehicle. The woman's children were waiting for her in the car. I hated that story when I first read it and I still hate it.

The songbirds, one dead and one alive, lay on the passenger's seat. At home, I unwrapped the male grosbeak and thought about what I could do to help him. I set him in a cardboard box in my kitchen. I buried the dead female in the garden.

Our friends would be arriving shortly. It was Independence Day and we were paddling. Raven would be paddling too if Margaret had not died. Part of me was wishing I had gone with him, but someone had to feed our farm animals and milk the cows. I wondered if I would be dishonoring Margaret's memory if I went to the river, and I decided that I would not be, that the river would be healing for me. I wished Raven could be there with us.

〜 Raven's sister was young, forty-six, a year younger than I. She had been diagnosed with kidney disease as a toddler, two years old, and had been tied to a dialysis machine most of her life, since she was eight. Everybody marveled at how long she had lived as a dialysis patient—she was a miracle. She had undergone three kidney transplants but none of them had succeeded.

The disease weakened her systems. It damaged her heart. An examination in early summer had shown a number of blockages, one at 90 percent and another at 95. Her doctors predicted that she would not survive open-heart surgery and suggested stents for the two worst blockages. It would be a simple procedure, they told her, thirty minutes, and she would be home the following day.

At 10:00 p.m. the evening before her surgery, Margaret telephoned. We were almost in bed. She sounded rushed, nervous, somewhat breathless. She wanted to check in, to tell her brother she loved him.

On the operating table the next morning, a Thursday, while doctors expanded the first artery with a small balloon, the artery burst. Bleeding internally, Margaret was rushed into emergency open-heart surgery. Doctors grafted a section of replacement artery on the broken one. Margaret was hooked to a respirator, to a heart assist, to a feeding tube. Doctors induced a coma. She had been given blood thinners during the initial stent surgery, and now she needed multiple blood transfusions.

She lived through surgery, through twenty-four hours of her chest open six to eight inches (in case the doctors needed to go back in). "It's touch and go," said the intensive-care nurses. "She's our worst patient." And, "If she survives, it'll be a long haul."

The bleeding stopped. Doctors began bringing Margaret out of the coma. A nurse asked her name and she spoke it. The respirator came out. Every day Margaret was better. We all thought she would pull through.

One night almost a week after the surgery, Margaret vomited and her heart stopped beating. Nurses performed CPR and brought her back. But her blood pressure was falling. The hospital counselor who makes that sort of call woke us at 1:30 in the morning to let us know. Two hours later he called to say she had died.

～ When I loaded my boat for the river, I was sleep-deprived. I was sad. I was second-guessing all that had happened. I had early that morning kissed my grieving husband goodbye at the airport terminal (why wasn't it called a nascent rather than a terminal?). I was worrying about an injured blue grosbeak back in my kitchen.

But there was hope for the bird. As I had packed lunch, the bird had flown from its cardboard box and clung to a beam in the peak of the ceiling.

～ I have made a decision you will not like. I am not going to tell you which tributary we were on, where we canoed that Independence Day, when I felt less independent than I've felt in my life, connected as I was to the eleven friends on the river with me, with my family, the farm, the life and death of birds, and when my heart was heavy with sadness.

I am not telling you which tributary we were on because it is yet pristine. The waterway is quite unlogged, naturally vegetated. No houses are built along the stretch of it, and I would hope that fear of flooding is not the only reason for this. I would hope that people would have the grace and the respect to leave this wild haven alone.

Most of south Georgia's sandbars are no longer white. Mostly they are yellow and brown, stained by the polluted, algal water that rises over them and then recedes, over and over. But this tributary's sandbars are white—actually a pure ivory—the blindingly bright color we used to know.

The water is true blackwater. It is the amber color of a glass of tea. It is a stream of gold. It is the long tresses of an auburn-haired woman. It is translucent.

This day, spring freshets had washed all trash away. We stowed trash bags and did not fill them, not until we reached the take-out landing where Fourth of July parties had left their messes.

Both the put-in and take-out are remote landings, known by locals only and not found in paddling books. The families camped at these places were local families.

Paddling as a local is very different from paddling as a visitor. In the person who is local, knowledge accumulates. His or her brain categorizes information in relation to other memories and stories, place-names and facts. Stories grow into each other, as the Virginia creeper grows into the birch, or the muscadine grows into the ash. A local, paddling her or his own river, is building a body of knowledge.

The visitor is building a list of experiences. When visitors come, other things get built also. Infrastructure to cater to them gets built.

I would prefer the locals keep this tributary to themselves and for any construction to be inner, immaterial, invisible.

The waterway (river, creek, tributary) was pure, yet wild, free of visible harm, flanked by cypress-knee forests, with water birch and swamp ash, but mostly lined with willow, black willow, billowing out into the stream and rooted in it, lapping from it. It was a blackwater tributary lined with black willow. The willows with their weary, drooping leaves matched my heavy heart.

Willows are trees with a love. If you have a weeping willow in your yard, you never let its branches touch the ground or somebody in your family will die. Never plant a willow. If you plant a willow it will search and search until it finds your water supply and then it will wrap itself around the pipe and choke off your water. A willow will not care if you thirst to death.

As we paddled, yellow-billed cuckoos clucked high in the cypress, as if children were playing with clackers, marbles on each end of a string. I call them rain crows, because their summer clucking gets more intense when the sky clouds. A barred owl lofted over the water. A mother mallard hid her ducklings among willows on a sandbar. I saw a great blue heron, once so common that if you saw one, you never thought twice about it—"There's the old preacher of the swamp," you'd say. Now it's increasingly rare. I saw a little blue and some greats. I saw killdeer on a sandbar.

Someone's cell phone rang and I was annoyed. Someone else checked a text message. With cell phones in pockets, now those who ranged ahead could contact those of us who lagged behind. I hated the idea of that. I am so fond of the ancient exchange of information, a knowing without words.

At rock shoals we got out to swim and float, up and down, back up and down. We ate lunch on a sandbar, under willows. After lunch I raced to get out front so I could be alone and see wildlife. Not that I do not enjoy my wonderful friends. But I wasn't very good company, exhausted as I was from the decisions, the misgivings, the sadness. Thinking of Margaret, I couldn't concentrate on conversation. I couldn't think of questions to ask.

What I needed was to watch the amber water sliding past the ivory sandbars under a high blue sky. I needed the peace of wildness.

That's one reason we go to rivers. We go to lay our burdens down, to refuel ourselves, to fill our eyes with beauty, to enter the unchanging, to experience metaphorical time. We go to be transformed.

When I got home, the blue grosbeak was flying around the kitchen, window to window, leaving chalky droppings on counters and floor. I cornered him and cupped my hands around him against the glass of one window. He squawked like a madman, then stilled and lay quiet in my hands. I was present in the moment. I was fully alive to the bird whose tiny heart beat between my fingers, alive to the room, to vegetables waiting on the counter to be processed into pickles and salsa and suppers, to the sunlight outside.

I carried my beautiful burden to the back door.

I wanted him to stay in my hand a long time, looking at me. I wanted him to stay, to live on my deck, to eat from my hand. He graced the laboriousness of my days. I might never hold another grosbeak. I wanted him to fly up and perch on my shoulder, to preen against my shirt. I did not want to let him go.

But my life was not wild enough for him. I could not care for him in the wild way he needed. I could only bring him into a human life, which would have been death for him. I knew when I opened my hand he would not pause. He would be gone. And so I was slow to open my palm. I wanted him to hear me crying out to him in my own strange language, to feel my love for him.

The blue grosbeak made a faltering flight fifty feet to Indian corn we'd planted that, because of drought, had not done much. When I turned back inside, the bird was clinging to a stunted tassel.

How many ways can I say this? All we have are moments. All we have are scenes by which to define our entire existence. These moments mark our lives, our passages through life, our paddles down the rivers of life. If we are not paying attention to them—if we're buried in our devices and our burdens—if we're not taking notes—we miss them.

When I am dying, reevaluating my life, I would like to remember only these moments, those in which no clocks are ticking, in which I am aware of my excruciating and increasing vulnerability, in which I am so grateful for my lot in life that I could fall prone to the ground, overwhelmed with gratitude, moment by moment by moment.

My life has been saved in moments.

In moments, my life has been made worthwhile.

CHAPTER 14 *Sancho Panza*

I am sitting alone at the mouth of Sancho Panza Creek, looking across at Sancho Panza beach and the mouth of the Altamaha River. Farther beyond are Egg Island, Egg Island bar, and Wolf Island. On the bars behind me are all kinds of shorebirds—armadas of brown pelicans, willet, sandpipers, seagulls, terns, oystercatchers. Vast sandflats all around are rippled with the waves of the most recent tide.

Here in the spring horseshoe crabs lay their eggs. Red knots pause in their long migrations. Bald eagles nest nearby.

Now, the tide is going out, but the creekbed will never be empty enough to cross. I don't think so, anyway. But we'll see. I'm going to sit here and see.

A cloud parade over the Altamaha follows the river inland. Stacia Hendricks, naturalist on Little St. Simons Island, where I am, explained it to me this morning. The water is warmer over the river, and so clouds gather in a line. We saw it this morning, she and I, as we kayaked Mosquito Creek, listening to marsh wrens and clapper rails, rasps of hidden seaside sparrows, gurgles of grackles, and overhead, ascensions of migrating tree swallows.

I borrowed a beach cruiser, deployed myself with a bottle of sunscreen and another of repellent, and pedaled alone the startlingly beautiful, dreamily wild island, all the way to Sancho Panza and the mouth of the Altamaha. The island is a work of art, a maritime collage of live oak, palmetto, Spanish moss, red cedar, old-growth slash pine, and cabbage palm, twisting and writhing in the constant influence of sea and wind. Here and there a dead red bay darkens the understory with a brown furor.

I love this bicycle. I laugh out loud with the joy of riding it. My bicycle back home says *work*. It says, *This is not a movie theater, why do you need an easy chair?* It says, *Get low for wind resistance, little tires are faster, you've got places to go.* But the beach cruiser says, *Have a good time. Cruise a little.* With wide tall handlebars it says, *Just step back if you want to stop.* It says, *Ride standing if you want. Or sit down on this wonderful wide seat. You are far far away. Enjoy life. Sail.*

Yesterday I pedaled with Raven to Myrtle Pond on the island, and his rear tire quit turning. We left the bike for a truck to retrieve and rode back to the lodge on one bicycle, taking turns pumping and steering or sitting on the seat, legs out, balancing and holding on for dear life. That was crazy joy.

The beach is covered with broken coquina (also whelk, sand dollar, and oyster shell) that crunch underfoot. An occasional olive shell can be found.

When I am far enough away that I know no one will hear or see me, even through binoculars, I talk to myself—usually in a British accent, I don't know why—not holding conversations but speaking what sounds to me like lines of poetry that will never get written. And I sing, I am the world, I am the trees, I am the clouds, I am the weeds, changing pitches and tunes and rhythms at will, thinking that it's not half-bad but knowing I'll not remember any of it.

I go and go, until I reach the last point of Sancho Panza beach, where the creek flows into the ocean and where the tide operates. Stacia told me this morning on the way back from the canoe launch that she saw a map of Little St. Simons Island from the 1880s and that it is one-third bigger now. It has been built up by accretion, sediment coming out of the Altamaha. I feel as if I have entered the heart of the world. My river made all this.

The Altamaha is a stem and at its mouth is an exquisite flower, and that flower is an island, Little St. Simons. The Altamaha nourishes the island. It feeds it, nutrients and minerals and microorganisms, which explains the swarming, crowning, spangling, breaching divinations of life found at its mouth. Black skimmers, royal terns, Wilson's plovers.

Little St. Simons is a baby right whale, nursing at its mother's teat, thriving on the dark milk of the Altamaha.

Here are some of the most beautiful things I've ever seen, in an openness that makes my psyche happy, the ancient human within me able to watch for predators. I am returned to a cradle of civilization, where my species again takes to two legs and begins to walk, and hope, and love, and desire, and crave, and travel, and desire what they see as they travel, which is more than they had when they stayed put.

In my wildest dreams I am lost among the dunes and the waves.

Finally I am inside, not outside. I am inside the world, with dragonflies, with willets and terns, with a train of clouds along the river—white, flat-bottomed, puffy on top, like little blue-tinged meringues. The tide is almost at its lowest, the creek is getting quiet.

I am the face of devotion. I am a worshipper at the feet of all we know of God manifest, which is creation.

I decide to cross the creek. I wait until the creek is still as ice. I take off my pants, fold them in my backpack, lift my bike high and slowly begin across the salt sea. Concerned about oysters, I keep my shoes on. My heart is pounding like a sledgehammer. I know how foolish this is. I am far, far, far away from any help. I'm on a remote beach of a wild island, where the Altamaha River empties into the Atlantic. I don't know how deep the salt creek is.

On the other side of Sancho Panza is a trail home. If I can get over to it, I won't have to go back the way I came. I can make a large circle.

I make my way across a wide mudflat to a shallowness that used to be the bottom of a creek. Slowly, step by step, watching for deep holes and being careful of any current, I make my way across, past oysters and tidepools, past sand dollars and coquina, across the corrugated bottom of the sea.

I make it to the other side.

CHAPTER 15 *Delta*

I am a speck in the life of this river. I am a blink in the long eye of history that stares us down. Before long I too will be gone, into the ground, with only a book left behind as proof that I loved the place where I existed, the place in which I was born and for most of my life chose to live. I will die and be buried, hopefully, a mile or two from the river that was as if my own backbone, and my grave will grow thick with grass. The swamp chestnut oak will drop its stiff, lobed leaves all over me.

For eleven thousand years, at least, people have lived here, first those we call natives because they were not European, as I am. They did not arrive by boat, as most Europeans did. They arrived on foot or by horse; and we, of course, have a strange and conflicted belief that the person who arrives by the most complicated conveyance gets to be boss.

Hernando de Soto, a Spaniard, came through in the 1500s. The French wandered near. Revolutionary soldiers gathered along Old River Road, a mile from where I now live, on which the Confederate Army and the Union Army also marched. Nearby were a school, a church, and a stage stop for the now defunct village of Altamaha, Georgia. It dropped mail and passengers in the 1800s.

On this land, up and down this river, people like me with dreams, with preferences, with raven hair whose color slowly seeps to gray, were born, lived, and died. Some of them left evidence of their passions, as did Lawrence Pearson, who in 1850 built the house I now live in, on a farm in southern Tattnall County that we call Red Earth, and whose esteem for wood and care for beauty are daily in evidence.

De Soto is gone. The Bartrams, elder and younger, are gone. Muir is gone.

The last steamboat captain is gone. His first mate is gone. The last rafthand is gone. The stagecoach drivers are gone.

Brainard Cheney rose and fell, as did Bill Haynes, Carolyn Hodges, and Milton Hopkins.

Countless fishermen and fisherwomen who loved sitting on the cut banks, or in their small and tidy boats on the steel-gray waters of the Altamaha, stringing out a line, are gone. The fisherpeople on the river today, a Friday in July in the year 2010, will soon be gone, others to take their place.

We people come and go, live and die, build and tear down, fight and love, kill and birth, enjoy ourselves or not, suffer or not.

What I grieve are the lost stories—commonplace sights and accounts of oddities, loves made and lost, departed sons, burdens borne, news that caused a person to sing. I am less sad that the stagecoach driver is gone than that his stories are gone. "I was only one of the fallen," wrote Linda Hogan, "in a lineage of fallen worlds and people."

I walk out to the paved road, Old River, overland trail used first by natives: I will sit all day and not see a stagecoach, pulled by four thirsty horses, gallop up to the Altamaha, Georgia, post office in a thunder of hooves and creak of leather, and I will not see its passengers dismount for refreshment, a drink of water from Slaughter Creek (no longer drinkable—very undrinkable, in fact), and I will not hear the driver's boisterous talk with the Pearsons who ran the sawmill there, or hear one of the women's laughter ring out.

I am forlorn for the stories lost to the sunset, lost to the horizon, lost to the night, permanently lost.

Once my farmer neighbor Winton Miles told me a strange story. "Did you hear about the Indian woman?" he said. "I'll tell you just how it was. When the government ran the Indians out of here, they thought they got them all. One stayed on this creek, Bay Creek, down near the swamp. She escaped the soldiers and hid out. She lived in the woods for many years—she was the only one left. She would stay in the woods until she nearly perished to death, then she got so hungry and weak that she had to come out. People had sentiments for her and would help her. She was old and frail-looking. She was small in stature. Old Man Moody told me about it. He said she would come out. He would help her get up food. The way he and the others talked they didn't know where she lived."

Were my imagination greater I would grant stories to the souls lost to history. Were I able to hear with my bones I would know the underside of their colossal silence. I would channel them.

We are each born afresh, to create afresh, to make logic of whatever order we have entered, which is always changing. The wiregrass flats, the ancient pine forests, the swamps full of swollen-base trees, the nests of the kites, the brilliant whiteness of the sandbars—all these are gone or almost gone. And I must make order of the pine plantations, my neighbors' trailer homes, the smell of chicken shit from industrial broiler houses, the pollution, the hate mail.

Such is the nature of history. Its truth fades. In the moment of an event, in the presence of the happening, truth is possible, in black and white. But when a moment is over, the truth of that moment begins to fade, to gray, to light gray, and all that is left are the stories passed from mouth to mind to mouth to mind, on and on. The truth becomes wide, diverse, multicolored, branching, diverging, like a delta.

As I paddle with my friends, old and new, the 137 miles of this river and the additional miles of its tributaries, all I know is what I see. What happened before my time is what I was told, and even then the stories told to me and those I read are sometimes at odds with each other, at cross-purposes. Such is the nature of our lives.

Therefore, history is interesting but I think what matters most is this moment. This moment of the river matters to me, and it matters to you because this is a moment I am living for you. This is a story I am writing for you, full of moments that are also yours. Wherever you are, on your river, the moment matters.

What doesn't fade is the setting, the place, the water. For twenty million years it has not faded, this vehicle of mystery, keeper of lost stories, avenue of secrets, course of history. This eternal fount.

Now is the moment to know it.

O river. Friend river. Some of your stories have been set free.

Altamaha River Lands in Conservation

(chronological, number of acres)

Altamaha Wildlife Management Area, 1957, 1959	12,478
Bullard Creek WMA, 1961	8,442
Wolf and Egg Islands (Savannah Refuge), 1969	4,572
Big Hammock Natural Area, 1972	801
Lewis Island Natural Area (Altamaha WMA), 1972	5,633
Big Hammock WMA, 1973, 1989	5,566
Altamaha Waterfowl Management Area–Phillips, 1973	730
Hofwyl-Broadfield Plantation, 1974	1,268
Altamaha-Rayonier Area (Altamaha WMA), 1977	1,331
Cathead Tract (Altamaha WMA), 1982	1,021
Cathead Creek, 1992	752
Audley Farms Tract (Altamaha WMA), 1994	324
Griffin Ridge WMA, 1996	5,616
Long County DOT Mitigation, 1996	1,300
Carr's Island, 1996	367
Montgomery DOT Mitigation, 1997	898
Potosi Island (Altamaha WMA), 1998	1,945
Tillman Tract (Big Hammock WMA), 1998	581
International Paper & The Timber Company Conservation Easement, 2000	1,223
Long County DOT Mitigation, 2000	3,970
Moody Forest Natural Area (DNR/TNC owned), 2000	4,368
Penholloway Swamp WMA, 2005	4,270
Clayhole Swamp WMA, 2005	5,243
Townsend WMA Conservation Easement to DNR, 2006	4,345
Townsend WMA, 2006	2,369
Penholloway Trade Lands Conservation Easement, 2006	373
Penholloway Trade Lands Conservation Easement, 2006	313

The Lost 1,000 LLC Conservation Easement, 2006	1,010
Williams Trust Tract—Townsend WMA, 2007	202
IP-Townsend Bombing Range—DOT Tract	1,709
Ft. Barrington/Long Branch Farms CBT Tract, 2007	385
IP-Townsend Bombing Range—USMC Easement, 2008	10,687
Ft. Barrington/Long Branch Farms Tract, 2008	4,162
Ft. Barrington Club Conservation Easement, 2008	1,359
Murff Tract, 2009 & 2010	14,091
Walker Lake, part of Townsend Wildlife Management Area, 2011	1,080
TOTAL	114,784

This list includes only land protected in the immediate Altamaha River corridor and not elsewhere in the watershed. Many thanks to The Nature Conservancy for completely funding and managing some of these tracts, and for assisting in the protection of the majority of the others.

This list was compiled by the Altamaha Bioreserve Project of The Nature Conservancy of Georgia, especially Christine Griffiths, Christi Lambert, and Alison McGee.

Protect and Preserve Our River

- Oppose water withdrawal of rural rivers for Atlanta's usage. Support and practice water conservation.
- Boycott cypress garden mulch. Stay out of stores that sell cypress mulch.
- Oppose the contamination of the Altamaha waters by industry.
- If you are a farmer, make sure the chemical fertilizers and pesticides you use on your fields are not polluting the river. Be especially aware of siltation, caused by erosion and runoff. Don't lose your good dirt. Transition to organic agriculture.
- Avoid lawn and garden chemicals, some of which wind up in our waterways (and in our food).
- If you cut timber, leave ample stream buffers. (The thirty feet recommended is not sufficient.) Practice selective cutting instead of clear-cutting.
- If you are a logger, become known for obeying Best Management Practices. Become a sustainable timber harvester.
- Never timber a wetland.
- If you are a builder, don't use cypress. The tree cannot be sustainably harvested at this point in the history of the earth.
- Stash litter securely in your boat, vehicle, or backpack until you can get to a trash can.
- Obey fishing regulations.
- Keep only the fish you can use and release all others.
- Fish barbless.
- Report fish and wildlife violations.
- Don't disturb or feed wildlife.
- Never kill a wading bird, for any reason.
- Never disturb the nest of a wild bird.
- Don't collect wild plants (unless the area is slated for destruction) or mussels.

- Don't release exotic plants or animals.
- When you finish using the children's loaner vest that you borrow from the nice kiosk, put it back.
- Keep livestock out of the river and its streams.
- Don't dump motor oil or chemicals in storm drains, in flowing water, or on the ground. Recycle them properly.
- Dispose of wild game carcasses away from streams and ponds.
- Get to know the sandhills and protect them from development and destruction.
- Snags and submerged rocks provide substrates for riverbottom life and cover for fish. Leave them alone.
- If trees must be removed from stream banks, *cut, don't pull* them. There's sediment and then there's sediment.
- Be the keeper of whatever place you live.

Resources

Altamaha River Bioreserve, The Nature Conservancy of Georgia
   Safeguarding this important river system through scientific study,
   landowner collaborations, and direct acquisitions.
PO Box 484
Darien, Ga. 31305
912.437.2161

Altamaha Riverkeeper
   Protecting and restoring the habitat, water quality, and flow of the
   mighty Altamaha from its headwaters in the Oconee, Ocmulgee, and
   Ohoopee to its terminus in the Atlantic Coast.
PO Box 2642
Darien, Ga. 31305
912.437.8164
www.altamahariverkeeper.org

Altamaha River Partnership
   Representing eleven counties working to promote the river
   as a great destination.
www.altamahariver.org

Center for a Sustainable Coast
   Working to improve the responsible use, protection, and conservation of
   coastal resources—natural, historic, and economic.
221 Mallery St. Suite B
St. Simons Island, Ga. 31522
912.638.3612
www.sustainablecoast.org

Georgia River Network
Working to ensure a clean water legacy by engaging and
empowering Georgians to protect and restore our rivers from the
mountains to the coast.
126 South Milledge Ave. Suite E3
Athens, Ga. 30605
706.549.4508
www.garivers.org

The Nature Conservancy of Georgia
Preserving the plants, animals and natural communities that
represent the diversity of life on Earth by protecting the lands and
waters they need to survive.
1330 W. Peachtree St. Suite 410
Atlanta, Ga. 30309
404.873.6946
www.nature.org/wherewework/northamerica/states/georgia

Nongame Conservation Section, Wildlife Resources Division
Georgia Department of Natural Resources
Managing Georgia's native diversity of nongame animals, rare plants and
natural habitats through education, research and management, while also
striving to increase public enjoyment of these natural resources.
2070 US Hwy. 278 SE
Social Circle, Ga. 30025
770.918.6411
www.gadnr.org

Project Orianne
A wildlife conservation organization dedicated to conserving
rare reptiles, especially the range-wide conservation of the eastern
indigo snake and its habitat.
579 Highway 441 South
Clayton, Ga. 30525
706.212.0112
www.projectorianne.org

Members of the Altamaha River Partnership

Baxley-Appling County Board of Tourism
305 W. Parker St.
Baxley, Ga. 31515
912.367.7731
www.baxley.org

Brunswick & The Golden Isles Visitors Bureau
4 Glynn Ave.
Brunswick, Ga. 31520
800.933.2627, 912.265.0620
www.comecoastawhile.com

City of Jesup, Georgia
162 E. Cherry St.
Jesup, Ga. 31546
912.427.1313
www.jesupga.gov

Darien-McIntosh County Chamber of Commerce
105 Ft. King George Dr.
Darien, Ga. 31305
912.437.6684
www.visitdarien.com

Glynn County Board of Commissioners
Historic Courthouse
701 G St.
Brunswick, Ga. 31520
912.554.7111
www.glynncounty.org

Greater Tattnall Chamber of Commerce
120 Brazell St.
Reidsville, Ga. 30453
912.557.6323
www.tattnall.com

Hazlehurst-Jeff Davis Board of Tourism
95 E. Jarman St.
Hazlehurst, Ga. 31539
912.375.4543
www.hazlehurst-jeffdavis.com

Montgomery & Toombs County Chamber of Commerce
PO Box 362
Mt. Vernon, Ga. 30445
912.583.4676
www.toombsmontgomerychamber.com

Telfair County Chamber of Commerce
9 E. Oak St.
McRae, Ga. 31055
229.868.6365
www.telfairco.org

Vidalia Tourism Council
100 Vidalia Sweet Onion Dr.
Vidalia, Ga. 30474
912.538.8687
www.vidaliaga.com

Wayne County Board of Tourism
101 E. Cherry St.
Jesup, Ga. 31546
912.427.3233
www.waynetourism.com

Wheeler County Chamber of Commerce
6 West Railroad Ave.
Alamo, Ga. 30411
912.568.7808
www.wheelercounty.org

Bibliography

Cheney, Brainard. *Lightwood*. Boston: Houghton Mifflin, 1939.

Cheney, Brainard. *River Rogue*. Boston: Houghton Mifflin, 1942.

Goff, John H. *Placenames of Georgia*. Edited by Francis Lee Utney and Marion R. Hemperley. Athens: University of Georgia Press, 1975.

Greene, Melissa Fay. *Praying for Sheetrock: A Work of Nonfiction*. Cambridge, Mass.: Da Capo, 2006.

Groover, Robert Long. *Sweet Land of Liberty: A History of Liberty County, Georgia*. Roswell, Ga.: W. H. Wolfe, 1987.

McGregory, Jerrilyn. *Wiregrass Country*. Jackson: University Press of Mississippi, 1997.

Morrison, Carlton A. *Running the River: Poleboats, Steamboats, and Timber Rafts on the Altamaha, Ocmulgee, Oconee, and Ohoopee*. St. Simons Island, Ga.: Saltmarsh Press, 2003. Based on a master's thesis at the University of Georgia, 1970, and with an introduction by Delma Presley.

Murphy, Reg. "The Easy Ways of the Altamaha." *National Geographic*, January 1998.

Presley, Delma E. *Project RAFT Festival Handbook*, April 1982.

Ray, Janisse. "Waiting for the Tide: Creating an Environmental Community in Georgia." *Orion Afield*, Summer 1999.

Ray, Janisse, ed. *Moody Forest: A Local History of Heart Pines, Spider Lilies, Old-Growth Cypress and Blackberry-picking along the Altamaha River of Appling County, Georgia, and the True Story of a Family's Extraordinary Dedication to Big Woods*. Reidsville, Ga.: Wildfire Press, 2007.

Walker, Jane. *Widow of Sighing Pines*. N.p.: n.p., 2002. (Copies may be ordered from PO Box 357, McRae, Ga., 31055.)

Gratitude

In memory of
Charley Joe Ray, 1900–1977
William G. Haynes Jr., 1908–2001
Carolyn Kuebler Hodges, 1938–2000
and
Milton Newton Hopkins, 1926–2007

I thank Christa Frangiamore Hayes for petitioning me so many years ago to write this book. I am grateful for her wonderful ideas and lasting friendship. Many thanks to Craig and Diana Barrow of the Wormsloe Foundation for their support of this volume.

I thank the good folks of the University of Georgia Press, especially Laura Sutton and John Joerschke, who oversaw the project; Nicole Mitchell and Dorinda Dallmeyer, whose support was boundless; John McLeod, who marketed it; Sydney Dupre; Kathi Morgan; and Judy Purdy, who got it all going. Molly Thompson's brilliance as a copyeditor is evident on every page of this book. Deborah Reade is a fine mapmaker. I thank colleagues John Tallmadge and Lauret Savoy for their thorough and wise edits to the manuscript.

Photographer Nancy Marshall took on the project of photographing the river with elegance and aplomb. I thank her very much for her spirit of collaboration and for her inspiring work. I am grateful for the chance to work with her. I am in gigantic debt to the following people, who assisted, guided, or inspired me, or shared their studies and stories: Dennis Blanton, Phyllis Bowen, John Bozeman, Bob Brannen, Dave Brown, Jackie Carter, Susan Cerulean, Crawfish Crawford, Scott Coleman, Sharon Collins, Lisa Crews, Robert DeWitt, Meredith Drury, Ann Singer Eason, Giana Eden, John Eden, Charlie Ford, Mac Herring, Neill Herring, James Holland, Dorset Hurley, Christine Griffiths, Christa F. Hayes, Stacia Hendricks, Hugh Joiner, Martha Joiner, Philip Juras, Eugene Keferl, Ann Ingerson,

Shelly Lakly, Christi Lambert, John Lane, Brent Martin, Chuck Martin, Alison McGee, Winton Miles, Carlton Morrison, Dink NeSmith (a gracious host at Whaley Lake), Carol Nourse, Hugh Nourse, Delma Presley, Carlin Joshua Ray, Dell and Rita Carter Ray, Franklin and Lee Ada Ray, Stephen Ray, Constance Riggins, Alan Roach, Jack Sandow, Patti Sandow, Deborah Sheppard, Frankie Snow, Leta Mac Stripling, Betsy Teter, Chris Trowell, Jane Walker, and Tommie Williams.

Matt Elliot, Jason Wiesniewski, Shan Cammack, Tim Keyes, Tom Patrick, and all the fabulous people in the Nongame Conservation Section of the Georgia Department of Natural Resources put all their resources at my disposal. The chief, Mike Harris, was vital. I thank them for studying wild Georgia and for educating us about the needs of our wild creatures. They are holding the line. It is an immense job and I am grateful to them.

For over a decade I have been associated with a community of colleagues in the Altamaha Riverkeeper, whose devotion to this river system and its people is evident in long hours spent organizing, planning, and executing. This group includes Taylor Barnhill, Bryce Baumgartner, Bruce Berryhill, Sally Bethea, Chandra Brown, Don Carson, Richard and Elise Creswell, Robert DeWitt, Ben Emanuel, Wright and Dusty Gres, Gabriel Hamon, Len Hauss, Neill Herring, James Holland, Cecil and Sandy Hudson, Christi Lambert, Marilyn Lanier, Sandy Layton, Susan Murphy, Constance Riggins, Gordon Rogers, Jack and Patti Sandow, Deborah Sheppard, Albert Way, Dianna Wedincamp, Jon Wilson, Mary Ellen Wilson, and Whit Wright.

I thank the landowners, up and down the watershed, who are not cutting the river swamps that they own, who are leaving the big trees, which will keep us alive in the hot times to come. Thanks to Hank and Wendy Paulson, for falling in love with Little St. Simons. I thank those who are putting conservation easements on their land, in order both to get tax credits and to preserve this beautiful and beleaguered country of ours. I thank everyone who is cutting water consumption, so that we lighten pressures on this most precious of elements; and I thank everyone who is not simply working toward sustainable sources of energy but also laboring to use resources more efficiently and carefully.

My deep and lasting gratitude goes to Michael Cichon, M.D.; Susan Ganio, R.N.; and their staff, who devoted themselves to helping me heal from chronic Lyme disease. I thank Elaine Cichon and the Clinic of Angels for financial support. Lee Arnold and the entire staff of Vidalia Medical Associates are to be highly commended. Their warmth and kindness sustained me through some rough days.

In addition, I am very, very grateful to Stephen King, Margaret Morehouse, and all at the Haven Foundation; and Lisa Collier Cool and Trustees of the American Society of Journalists and Authors Charitable Trust for a grant from the Writers Emergency Assistance Fund.

My strong and handsome son, Silas Ray-Burns, was at my side during much of this narrative and in my heart during all of it. His middle name should have been Altamaha, because its water is his blood also. I thank him.

My love and gratitude for my husband, Raven Waters, grows with time. He is my leaning-post and my resting-place, and is present in every word of this book.

Note: Some names have been changed to protect identities.

Acknowledgments of
Nancy Marshall, Photographer

With appreciation to Christa Frangiamore Hayes for having the idea for a project with Janisse; to Deborah Sheppard, Captain Sheryl Schooley, James Holland, and Neill Herring of Altamaha Riverkeeper for their generous hospitality and river-guiding; and to John McWilliams for advice and companionship.

I dedicate these photographs to the memory of Joseph Terry Kennedy (December 8, 1945–May 13, 2010), a friend who was like a brother to me. He was a masterful photographer, a compelling writer, and a storyteller with a gift for living in the moment. He was completely at home in the wild.